Deep Curriculum Alignment

Creating a Level Playing Field for All Children on High-Stakes Tests of Educational Accountability

Fenwick W. English
Betty E. Steffy

Rowman & Littlefield Education
Lanham • New York • Toronto • Oxford

Published in the United States of America
by Rowman & Littlefield Education
A Division of Rowman & Littlefield Publishers, Inc.
A wholly owned subsidiary of The Rowman & Littlefield Publishing Group, Inc.
4501 Forbes Boulevard, Suite 200, Lanham, Maryland 20706
www.rowmaneducation.com

PO Box 317
Oxford
0X2 9RU, UK

British Library Cataloguing in Publication Information Available

Library of Congress Cataloging-in-Publication Data

English, Fenwick W.
  Deep curriculum alignment : creating a level playing field for all children on
high-stakes tests of educational accountability / Fenwick W. English, Betty E. Steffy.
    p. cm.
  Includes bibliographical references and index.
  ISBN 0-8108-3971-7 (alk. paper)
    1. Curriculum planning—United States. 2. Educational tests and measurements—Social
aspects—United States. 3. Educational accountability—United States. I. Steffy, Betty E.
II. Title.

LB2806.15 .E52 2000
375'.001'0973—dc21

                                                                00-051613

⊗™ The paper used in this publication meets the minimum requirements of
American National Standard for Information Sciences—Permanence of Paper
for Printed Library Materials, ANSI/NISO Z39.48-1992.
Manufactured in the United States of America.

Contents

Introduction

> When one considers in its length and in its breadth the importance of this question of the education of a nation's young, the broken lives, the defeated hopes, the national failures, which result from the frivolous inertia with which it is treated, it is difficult to restrain within oneself a savage rage.
>
> —Alfred North Whitehead (1959)

 $\mathcal{A}$ cross the landscape of America, high-stakes testing continues to leave in its cyclonic path defeated hopes and broken lives. It has been estimated that between 114 and 320 million tests are given per year in American schools (Madaus and Kellaghan, 1992, p. 126). Like Alfred North Whitehead (1959), we have worked along this highway for nearly three decades, bolstering the shaken confidence of dedicated teachers and administrators by showing that nothing is "wrong" with them, and certainly nothing "deficient" or "inferior" about their children.

If ever there was a misguided policy initiative, it is that somehow high-stakes testing can drive quality into the public schools by ratcheting up the consequences for not doing well on them. This approach is nothing more than mass-legislated inspection decried and condemned by the father of quality, W. Edward Deming (1986), who said that "Inspection to improve quality is too late, ineffective, costly" (p. 28).

Legislators, and those who advise them, appear to believe that the solution is to simply scare the daylights out of teachers and administrators so that they teach better. Improvement means better test scores.

The confusion that such emphasis on tests creates in the minds of teachers and administrators is legion. The temptation to engage in drill and kill exercises is nearly overwhelming and drowns out even common sense.

When that impulse becomes dominant, we have the lobotomization of instruction. Instruction isn't just dumbed down, it becomes the ultimate bureaucratic iron cage: lifeless, mechanical, and cold.

But why then be concerned with curriculum alignment? Why not just work to rid the educational scene of the horrors of testing run amuck? First, we have strong doubts that—no matter what logic is presented to legislators—there will be any persuasive argument until too much money has been spent and the desired remedies have not been forthcoming. The only data that will ultimately be convincing is when high-stakes testing has failed to bring about long-lasting educational improvements in the public schools. We see a lot of short-term jumps in test scores, but whether such jumps can be longitudinally sustained is conjectural. Even if that becomes a reality, the question of whether such gains actually represent better education still won't have been answered.

Curriculum alignment works in any testing scenario. As a principle, it will work with forms of authentic assessment as well as other kinds of tests. As a matter of fact, we learned about alignment on the old authentic assessments developed in the early days of the Kentucky Education Reform Act (KERA), which very regrettably have since been abandoned because of the necessity of tying dollars to so-called results.

To those critics who say that curriculum alignment is simply teaching to the test, we smile because they are half right anyway. When performance is defined by the test instead of the curriculum, improving performance is not teaching the curriculum better, but teaching the content of the test better. This is the irony of using nonaligned tests as high-stakes measuring tools. Becoming a so-called high-performing school on a test that doesn't match any local curriculum requires matching the curriculum to be taught to the test in use. Teaching to the test is unavoidable. For schools that have high enrollments from children of poverty, there is little alternative. We've said in this situation there are no poor schools; there are only schools serving the poor.

Deep alignment is a comprehensive approach to teaching and learning that goes beyond any single measure of the curriculum taught or learned. It is broadly anticipatory of any form of assessment. It is based on what we call the doctrine of no surprises, that is, children will not be taken by surprise with any form of assessment because assessment is an integral part of the instructional program, not an add-on.

We have nothing but antipathy for those who use high-stakes testing to demean children of the poor and of color. We've met plenty of these closet racists: legislators, school board members, business and community leaders, and even tragically a few administrators, teachers, and academics, who corner you after learning about alignment and ask, "You don't really believe that *those children* can ever really do well on these tests, do you?" Their confusion between cultural differences and stupidity, as Joe Kincheloe (1999) has observed, has been confirmed with the test results (p. 245). Their prejudices are not easily shaken. To do so would not only mean re-examining those ingrained biases, but coming to see tests as tools that discriminate against the culturally different. Tests are a very far cry from being the culturally neutral and objective tools they are often touted to be. On this matter we believe Arthur Jensen (1980) is flat wrong. We quote his work in this book in a variety of places, but we have some very fundamental disagreements with the idea that tests are not biased. When such tests have historically advantaged children of wealth because of their access to cultural capital, we believe Jensen does not connect poverty (SES indicators) to race (Carnoy, 1999, p. 29; Milken, 2000, p. A34).

Poverty is not a random variable in America, where "1.6% of the population own 80 percent of all stock, 100 percent of all state and municipal bonds, and 88.5 percent of corporate bonds" (Lundberg, 1968, p. 144).

Finally, some may see a contradiction in our advocacy of (1) a true national exam based on a national curriculum, and (2) alignment to improve pupil scores in a system that is culturally oppressive. We answer these potential queries by saying that we see a national exam in terms of embracing and celebrating cultural diversity in a nation that is moving rapidly to becoming multicultural in its composition. The America of 2050 will be far different from the America of 1950. We also believe that the respective states have "muffed it" as far as putting into place the best (rather than the cheapest) form of assessment possible. Kentucky made a dramatic, brilliant, and courageous move toward authentic assessment, but gave it up mid-course.

Although we recognize that school systems have been and continue to exercise forms of domination that are culturally oppressive, alignment demonstrates that all children can learn and be successful. Alignment plants doubts in the minds of those who have believed the racist and sexist explanations for poor test scores. It does it right inside the system itself so that it can't be explained away as some utopian scheme advanced by fuzzy-headed liberals working in the ivory towers of academe.

Finally, we agree with the great organizer of poor communities, Saul Alinsky (1969), when he said:

> the status quo is your best ally if properly goaded and guided. I have also learned to avoid succumbing to a rationale which would permit me the escape of becoming a rhetorical radical and not a radical realist. (p. x)

This book is about the here and now and how to create a level playing field for all children so that the current system of schooling becomes fairer for everyone. But it is also about the future, a very different future. Because alignment works, there is a future worth working for: for all children of all people; and because we are different and our differences are recognized and celebrated, we are still one nation indivisible.

REFERENCES

Alinsky, S. (1969). *Reveille for radicals.* New York: Vintage.

Carnoy, M. (1999). *Globilization and educational reform: What planners need to know.* Paris, France: UNESCO: International Institute for Educational Planning.

Deming, E. (1986). *Out of the crisis.* Cambridge, MA: MIT Press.

Jensen, A. (1980). *Bias in mental testing.* New York: Free Press.

Kincheloe, J. (1999). *How do we tell the workers?* Boulder, CO: Westview.

Lundberg, F. (1968). *The rich and the super rich.* New York: Lyle Stuart.

Madaus, G. and Kellaghan, T. (1992). Curriculum evaluation and assessment. In P. Jackson (ed.) *Handbook of research on curriculum.* New York: Maxwell Macmillan International, 119–156.

Milken, M. (2000, September 5). Amid plenty, the wage gap widens. *The Wall Street Journal,* A34.

Whitehead, A. (1959). *The aims of education and other essays.* New York: Macmillan.

Facing the Scourge
of the Test Score Zeitgeist

*A*n editorial cartoon by Stahler (1999) in the Denver *Rocky Mountain News* shows a mother seated in a chair reading a bedtime story to her daughter. The caption reads: "And the little pig with the higher math and verbal lived happily ever after. The other two were swallowed up by the wolf" (p. 63A).

Public education in America finds itself in the continuing throes of the accountability movement where standardized or criterion-referenced test scores are widely used to frighten, shame, punish, or reward local school teachers and administrators (McGinn, 1999; Johnston, 2000). No other country in the world has been stung by the testing movement as hard as the United States has been (Paris, Lawton, Turner, and Roth, 1991, p. 13). The National Commission on Testing and Public Policy (1990) estimates that each year the equivalent of twenty million school days are consumed with American children taking tests. This figure doesn't even include the amount of time getting ready to take the tests!

The many manifestations of this movement are abetted by governors and presidential candidates taking positions regarding changing technology, teachers' salaries, the preparation of teachers, the perceived lack of rigor in the curriculum, and the inability of the schools to provide a meaningful, high-quality education for all students compelled to attend them.

Linn (2000) recounts why assessment and accountability have been so dominant in educational reform efforts in the last fifty years. They are:

- *Tests are cheap* compared to things like class size reduction or hiring more aides;

1

- *Tests can be externally mandated* rather easily compared to trying to change what happens in classrooms;
- *Tests can be quickly implemented* and within the terms of office of elected legislators, so that claims of improvement can be attached to candidate incumbency;
- *Test results are visible* and can be made into good media release;
- *Test results in the first years are usually positive,* enabling policymakers to make claims of improvement without really having to change much (p. 4).

The downside has been the persistent gap in test scores between children of poverty and color and those of the largely white, suburban schools. The gap (Jencks and Phillips, 1998) has been the spawning ground for the resurrection of flawed explanations of differences that cannot be erased by good schools and which are purported to be the result of Darwinian processes at work. One story is that "those children," usually African American or Hispanic, do poorly in schools because they lack the appropriate mental capacity of their white, largely European counterparts (Hernstein and Murray, 1994). Recent research, however, provides "no evidence for the genetic superiority of either race, but strong evidence for a substantial environmental contribution to the I.Q. gap between blacks and whites" (Nisbett, 1998, p. 101). Intelligence testing has been intimately connected with ideas of racism, amply illustrated in the history of the testing movement and its early assumptions (Gould, 1981; Lehman, 1999). According to Kincheloe (1999), "school leaders still have trouble understanding that the poor are not stupid. . . . Educators mistake lower socioeconomic class manners, attitudes, and speech for lack of academic ability" (p. 245).

On the other hand, politicians who play to the lowest common denominators whipsaw general public opinion because of the lack of a sophisticated audience. "The irony of the public demand for standardized test data is that it is based on blind faith in the accuracy of the data," note Paris, Lawton, Turner, and Roth (1991, p. 14). If one wants to have the voting public take a particular antidote seriously, one offers a simple solution to a complex problem. That is, one has to reduce the problem to a simple one (Paris, Lawton, Turner, and Roth, 1991; Linn, 2000). The fact that American test scores internationally are not as good as other less prosperous or powerful nations is a fact that cannot be easily explained by the lack of public attention or the support education receives in the United States (Baker, 1993; Stedman, 1994). Poor test scores internationally and nationally remain the Achilles' heel of anyone who tries to bring in "good news" about American education. Here are some of the themes that run through much of the rhetoric about the so-called deficits of public education today. We enumerate them here because we don't believe any of them deals with the real problem of low test scores, but they sound good on the surface. They are repeated enough on the nation's editorial pages and columns to enjoy a measure of plausibility in the public's mind. We refer to them as culprits.

Culprit 1: The Monopolistic and Inefficient Nature of Public Education

The first target of those desiring to "improve schools" is to point out that public education is a monopoly. As such, school boards, administrators, and teachers have no incentive to change for the better. It is argued that without the presence of competition, mediocrity will rule (Finn, 1991; Carnoy, 1999, p. 38). Lacking incentives to change, teachers, administrators, and school board members must be intimidated and bullied into changing by negative publicity surrounding test scores. The installation of a range of punishments includes licensure revocation, more work, which is portrayed as therapeutic (good for them), and outright shame. If schools cannot be changed, they must be replaced by strategies of attrition, that is, by embracing political actions, which cut off their funding and starve them into changing, or face a kind of permanent fiduciary death sentence.

Carnoy (1999) explains how tests have been used as political weapons in the battle to reduce teacher salaries and cut back public school financial support in order to give parents incentives to enroll their children in private schools (p. 61). In the name of efficiency, the battle over vouchers continues (see Gigot, 2000, p. A10; Reich, 2000, p. A26), and is supported by organs of international business such as the World Bank, the International Monetary Fund (IMF), the African Development Bank, the Asian Development Bank, and the Inter-American Development Bank. These institutions are interested in reducing the costs of public sector services and of education, which translates to larger class sizes and privatizing schooling (Carnoy, 1999; World Bank, 1995).

Carnoy (1999) cites the case of Cuba, whose test scores are consistently two standard deviations higher than comparable scores in Brazil, Chile, and Argentina, countries with higher per capita income. Cuban schools are operated by a highly centralized, authoritarian, socialist state in which competition is not permitted (p. 67). Cuba has also invested heavily in education. In 1992–1993, 23 percent of the national budget was spent on education. Cuba has a ratio of one teacher for every forty-two inhabitants, "the highest of any nation in the world" (McDonald, 2000, p. 44).

The accomplishment of Cuban education must be measured by the fact that in 1959 Cuba had nearly a million illiterate citizens (McDonald, 2000, p. 45). Three years later, Cuba had all but eliminated illiteracy in the entire population (Wald, 1978). Cuban authorities have used tests not as leverage to invest less in education, but as a way of investing more. This situation is quite a contrast to other Latin American countries and the United States where test scores have been used to reduce public support of schooling (Carnoy and Werthein, 1980; Carnoy and Torres, 1989).

Culprit 2: The Genetic Incapacity of Minority Children and Children of Color to Do Well in School

Poor test scores perpetuate the myth that children of color and/or poverty lack the ability to do well in school (see Kincheloe, 1999, pp. 237–261). They are not as able, not as motivated, their parents don't care about education, and the children have an innate, shallower capacity for education. Furthermore, they are prone to antisocial behavior and criminality. So-called scientific studies of I.Q. are advanced to support such theses. The continuing work of Arthur Jensen (1998) points to an I.Q. gap between blacks and whites of fifteen points in favor of whites. Jensen believes that such differences are genetic. In this, he fails to deal with cultural differences which are known to have an impact on I.Q. averages, such as the proclivity of white mothers to breast-feed their babies compared to black mothers who do not; the fact that black mothers are much more likely to give birth to underweight babies which affects I.Q. scores; and black mothers are less likely to make eye contact and talk to their babies than their white counterparts (Holt, 1998, p. A20). All of these are cultural practices and have nothing to do with genetic inheritance. Breast-feeding has an effect amounting to an I.Q. increase of ten points and talking to infants appears to have a large bearing on the future development of the brain.

Culprit 3: The Intransigence of Teacher Unions to Educational Reform

The bridge from resistant school boards and administrators to change to examining the teachers and their organizations is not a difficult one to construct. Myron Lieberman's (1997) exposé of the politics of teacher unions (both the NEA and the AFT) denigrates collective bargaining because it excludes other constituencies and is therefore antidemocratic. This posture is an astonishing confession for someone who advocated and participated in collective bargaining for nearly twenty years (see Lieberman, 1960).

Lieberman's about-face on this issue stems in part from the fantastic growth and power of teacher unions at the state level, and the fact that unions have worked hard to oppose various schemes relating to school privatization. Lieberman (1993) long ago concluded that public education was finished in its current form. Privatization, therefore, represents the possibility of more radical change being possible to save public education.

In their classic portrayal of types of organizations, Blau and Scott (1962) cast unions as mutual benefit associations (pp. 45–49) whose primary interest was that the membership be the main beneficiary of its activities. The two threats internally to this type of organization were (1) membership apathy, and (2) oligarchical control. Lieberman (1997) makes much of the high-roller salaries and fringe benefits NEA and AFT officers receive, as well as the huge bureaucracies they have assembled to carry out their work as "education's gravy train" (pp. 124–146). He is particularly critical of the AFT's war against contracting out some of Hartford, Connecticut's poor performing schools to a private firm, Education Alternatives, when the average teacher's salary was $58,800 not including fringe benefits (p. 117). Criticism of teacher unions is not new (see Braun, 1972) and we find that antagonism toward them because of their opposition to so-called reform naïve. A mutual benefit association will be opposed to any scheme that works to the detriment of its members. Why should teacher unions be any different from any other kind of union? Teacher unions will support educational reforms in which their members benefit. Unions are a fact of life. We know of several cases where areas of the curriculum would have been cut were it not for a board of education being obliged to abide by its contract with its teachers' union. Teacher union leaders are not opposed to change or reform. They will be opposed to change or reform that diminishes or undermines current benefits their members enjoy.

Carnoy (1999) also provides some perspective on Lieberman's criticisms. Carnoy notes that the strategy of the World Bank has been to privatize teacher markets, increase their workloads, and reduce their pay. "When teachers resist externally imposed reforms that worsen their conditions, their associations [i.e., unions] are characterized as the major obstacle to educational improvement" (p. 69).

Culprit 4: The Lack of Intellectual Rigor in Colleges of Education

Test scores are also used to define capacity at the university level. In this tautological scheme, the low SAT scores of students in colleges of education define them as less intellectually capable, even as (1) the SAT scores of students choosing to teach have increased, and (2) the SAT is a poor predictor of success as a teacher (see Berliner and Biddle, 1995, p. 106). The idea that colleges of education are places where the less-able students on university campuses can find a home is a myth. While criticisms about course content being "pap" are legion, the evidence today suggests otherwise (Berliner and Biddle, 1995, pp. 107–108). We deal with the shortcomings of colleges of education in chapter 5 of this book. We've worked in them on different university campuses for two decades. We have not found them the wild-eyed, liberal places they are reputed to be (see Finn, 1991, pp. 222–228). Rather, we agree with many of their academic critics (Giroux, 1988, p. 173; 1994, pp. 464–469; Macedo, 1994, p. 152); they are very conservative places and by default end up supporting the socioeconomic status quo because of the faculty's inability to grasp the relationship between how schools reproduce the inequities in wealth and class privilege and increase them under the mantle of false objectivity.

Henry Giroux's (1994) criticism of colleges of education is that for professors to deal with the idea that they are cultural workers preparing other cultural workers to reproduce the socioeconomic status quo flies in the face of their self-concepts that they are professionals scientifically preparing trainees in objective and neutral curricula (p. 464). The study of pedagogy is presented to aspiring teachers as emanating from the "scientific" fields of psychology and sociology and fails to deal with the structured silences about the politics that undergird such claims. To deal successfully with this larger understanding of sociopolitics would require a multidisciplinary approach focused on larger issues than methods and techniques dealing with motivation, technological applications, or instructional design and delivery issues. To believe that faculty in colleges of education could work on a multidisciplinary basis across departments poses an unbelievable obstacle. The promotion and tenure process works against colleagues with diverse views. There are orthodoxies of belief in colleges of education as everywhere on the university campus. Bucking the trend is not easy, and younger faculty are acutely sensitive about expressing opinions that deviate from their senior colleagues in very fundamental ways. In our sojourn at different universities, we have discovered a fundamental contradiction about university life. In a place where differences of opinion are supposed to be honored, one finds too often not only intellectual rigor mortis, but a virulent form of centrism about everything. Such rigidity was noted by Thomas Kuhn (1962, p. 24) in his study of paradigm changes.

> No part of normal science is to call forth new sorts of phenomena; indeed those that will not fit the box are often not seen at all. Nor do sci-

entists normally aim to invent new theories, and they are intolerant of those invented by others.

Education professors are no different from their counterparts in other schools and colleges at any large university campus. They are highly resistant to reexamining fundamental presuppositions about their research and their opinions. We support the view that colleges of education are too conservative in nearly every way to be places where prospective teachers and administrators can learn how to engage in education to advance social justice, which we believe is the real agenda for education in the twenty-first century.

Culprit 5: The Good 'Ole Boy Coaches Who Dominate School Leadership Positions

Low test scores perpetuate the perspective that educational leaders are of a lesser intellectual bent. Educational administration is perceived as the epitome of the "jock culture" and anti-intellectualism that pervade the ranks of principals and superintendents. One argument goes that the reason academic attainment is not honored in the schools is that too many school leaders are ex-coaches who survived in college through athletics and not academics. While jocks may understand how to backslap the public, they don't know how to, nor are they interested in dealing with, matters of curriculum and instruction.

Data on school superintendents gathered by Glass (1992) show that "the popular belief that superintendents are former physical education teachers and coaches is validated neither in the 1992 nor 1982 surveys. Most were social studies teachers, and many others were science, math, or English teachers" (pp. 19–20).

Contemporary test score pressures are part of the negative conditions in the public schools that have led to a nationwide shortage of administrators, which is expected to worsen in the years ahead. In an ironic twist of metaphors, Steinberg (2000) described the situation as follows:

> the principal has become as visibly accountable as a football coach, and must suffer the wrath of parents and state monitors if a school has a losing season, as measured by falling test scores. (p. 1)

Coaches are used to such pressures. Non-coaches are not. Perhaps coaching is one effective way of preparing school administrators in schools where test scores and game scores are ultimately the defining moments.

Culprit 6: The Lack of "Quality" in Schools Which Must Be Forcefully Inserted by Ratcheting Up the Consequences of Not Doing Well on State Tests

Low test scores and the general American fascination with them have given rise to high-stakes tests in which the consequences of not doing well become more and more odious. Various forms of "educational bankruptcy" have become common, where schools performing poorly on state-designed instruments are labeled "schools in crisis," with dire consequences to the principals and teachers in them. In some states, principals can be removed from office and teachers must take additional competency exams if their children do not perform as expected. The idea is that by ratcheting up standards and passing scores, education can be dragged onto higher levels of performance.

We think these "culprits" have little or nothing to do with poor test scores. Fixing them will not improve test scores because test scores are not caused by any of them. Some of the culprits are political mirages perpetuated by a continuing hostility to the idea of the common school as a place where all children find a place to learn about each other and to acquire the firsthand knowledge of the democratic experience. The American public school has long lived with its share of political enemies, among them those who are opposed to general tax revenues supporting a free public education for all, and those who desire a particular sectarian perspective to be imposed on everyone else. Americans are not bashful about saddling their schools with new social challenges, such as coping with the larger societal problem of AIDS and drugs. Using the schools for such ends may be convenient, but also serves to drive out patrons who resent the emphasis on nonacademics and who find the increasing exposure to such problems nonproductive and even vulgar.

SOME POPULAR MYTHS ABOUT TESTS

We also need to point out some obvious aspects of testing that are, well, not so obvious, even to those who should know better. Once school personnel are caught up in the powerful centrifugal forces of high-stakes testing and accountability, the pressures may become so intense that whatever may be left of "common sense" about them is lost or forgotten. We think these are important to understand.

Myth 1: Tests Are Neutral and Objective

We should begin by dispelling the myth that tests are neutral or objective tools of education. It's easy to lose sight of this fact in the impressive statistics that many tests generate, but the presence of computation often masks the subjectivity and values that are inherent in any test. Tests represent many decisions about what and who considers the content they embrace as important. Since there is no science of selecting curriculum content, the "stuff" that ends up in tests is not the product of some new form of value-neutral engineering. Nearly all curriculum content is selected by a form of consensus, some more democratic than others. The content included on most norm-referenced, standardized tests has been selected by a group of experts. Compared to the selection of textbook content, such decisions are determined by various commissions and studies, anthologies of facts, and concepts somebody or some group considers most valuable to learn in the area to be tested. Determining such consensus can be an arduous and controversial task, especially in the humanities (DelFattore 1992; Nash, Crabtree, and Dunn, 1997).

Consensus in a democracy is never a precise process and it is subject to all of the rough-and-tumble power politics that always surround important matters in a society. The bottom line is that somebody has to decide what is going to be included in a test. Such decisions are not plebiscites among the general population; they simply include what the largest group of stakeholders may think is the most important. The determination of test content is very much a process of elite decision making by those in a position to be influential within the very small circles in which these decisions are made. There are no scientific studies about this aspect of test development, that is, determining the realpolitik of creating the curriculum content that becomes the test content. This issue transcends matters of reliability and validity. They strike at the core of the question, "Of all the things children should know, why these?" or "What knowledge is of most worth?"

Myth 2: Tests Are Meritocratic Tools

The idea that tests embrace knowledge is decidedly too static to explain what is going on in schools today. We shall call the content of tests the designated and sanctioned cultural capital that they embrace (see Apple, 1979, p. 3; Bernstein, 1990, p. 78; Giroux, 1997, p. 6; Portes, 1999, p. 501). Cultural capital "involves ways of dressing, acting, thinking, or representing oneself" (Kincheloe, 1999, p. 222). Ways of thinking and acting involve the knowledge acquisition that most people believe is one of the functions of schooling. Without much cogitation, most Americans believe that all children have equal access to forms of cultural capital that make a difference on tests. Many Americans believe that most children line up at the same starting line in kindergarten, and have an equal shot at doing well in acquiring that cultural capital. If children are motivated, if they come from homes that value education, and if they persevere, they can rise to the top, or so the story goes. There is abundant evidence that this popular image is false. From the very beginning of their existence, I.Q. tests discriminated against children of the working classes (see Jensen, 1980, p. 367). What generates top scores on many norm-referenced, standardized tests is wealth—because money buys access to the forms of cultural capital that end up being used on tests. Peter Sacks (1997) quotes college board data that "show that someone taking the (SAT) can expect to score about thirty test points higher for every $10,000 in his parents' yearly income" (p. 27). A study completed in a 1997 Delaware school district (Boyd) at a large Delaware high school in which parental income was a known variable showed the following:

Lake Forest School District
SAT Scores for the 1996–1997 School Year (n=102)

Annual Family Income	SAT Test Takers		Percent		SAT 1 Verbal	SAT 1 Math
	Number	Percent	Male	Female		
Less than $10,000	5	7	60	40	436	508
$10,000–$20,000	6	8	50	50	475	533
$20,000–$30,000	11	15	73	27	448	477
$30,000–$40,000	18	21	56	44	489	453
$40,000–$50,000	13	17	38	62	461	458
$50,000–$60,000	9	12	22	78	478	448
$60,000–$70,000	8	11	87	13	493	518
$70,000–$80,000	5	7	80	20	572	580
$80,000–$100,000	2	3	50	50	No data	No data

The Lake Forest data clearly show a relationship between income and scores on the SAT. The extreme scores, very high and very low, show up on the verbal with some overlap by $10,000 increments in the mid-income ranges. The correlation on math scores is not as clear, with the lowest being a 446 in the income range $50,000–$60,000, yet this may be explained by a gender bias: 78 percent of the respondents in this range were female.

The data on norm-referenced, standardized tests is that they are not meritocratic tools. The evidence shows that they discriminate against children of the poor and children of color (Robinson and Brandon, 1994; Campbell, 1998; Lehman, 1999; Viadero and Johnston, 2000; Linn, 2000). These wealth-related variables, which consistently predict test score success, especially those that are not aligned to any specific curriculum, have little or nothing to do with what schools do. Especially in the industrial countries of the world, the less influence school factors have in affecting test scores and the more they are determined by socioeconomic factors (Stedman, 1994, p. 31). In such circumstances, test score results flow around the obvious socioeconomic fault lines. The best scores come from the wealthiest areas of town and the lowest scores come from the poorest areas of the same town. The use of norm-referenced, standardized tests on a statewide basis without alignment will follow the same fault lines. The highest scores will follow the money. There is nothing meritocratic about this unless one wants to argue that society has already taken a meritocratic configuration and the test scores are a reflection of these forces at work. But this is a social-Darwinian presentation that belies the continuation of privilege in the name of a false science. In a society where the *have nots* are continuously told that with application they could become the *haves,* their failures have to be viewed as personal shortcomings instead of flaws in the system itself. As long as the predictor variables of test scores remain wealth (sometimes called SES; see Carnoy, 1999, p. 29), race, and gender, there can be no meritocracy that is also not based on the same variables. A meritocracy should be free from these biases. In this sense, the political rhetoric of creating an educational system in which all children can find success of some sort irrespective of their race, gender, or social background falls far short of the reality of the tests in use. Given the current inequities in the access to cultural capital in the larger society that make up the stuff of most tests, no test can be an impartial, neutral, or unbiased source of information about a child (Darling-Hammond, 1997). They do so not because they are statistically flawed, but because the content they embrace is not accessible to all children equally. In short, it's not a fair world and tests do not ensure that it will become any fairer.

Myth 3: Tests Take the Politics Out of Education

The use of tests as political weapons has a long history in education. The father of American public education, Horace Mann, and his reformers used tests to wrest control of the schools from the Boston schoolmasters in the nineteenth century (Messerli, 1972, pp. 418–419). Decisions about test content are value based and ultimately political. The application of tests, from the classroom to a state education agency, is an expression of political power. The power to examine confers a position of status and authority. As more and more state education agencies take to expanding statewide tests over an increasing range of the school curriculum, the importance of local control and initiative passes from local boards of education to the state. Local boards of education are increasingly becoming factotums as the initiative has shifted from local to state domination of the curriculum (Johnston and Sandham, 1999).

Tests have also provided the respective state agencies with an agenda to expand their control without appearing to do so. We call this the "back door approach" to control. Many states have been reluctant to embrace a statewide curriculum because that would be too much of a direct assault on the tradition of local boards of education establishing the curriculum within a broad state framework. On the other hand, the idea that the state should establish a statewide assessment program in the name of fairness, economy, and comparability encounters considerably less political opposition. When the state attaches dire consequences to poor test performance and raises the stakes to include state takeover of poor performing schools, the state's control of curriculum is cemented through the back door of test content.

In the application of testing programs, some groups are advantaged and others disadvantaged. The winners are state agencies. The losers are local boards of education. Local control of the curriculum is dying on the vine. The energy that most school system administrators and teachers spend on trying to meet state minimums leaves little room for attention to whatever else remains. What gets tested is what counts. What isn't tested doesn't count and therefore isn't as important. What has been lost in the frenzy to comply with high-stakes testing is the idea of a balanced curriculum which includes art, music, poetry, drama, and in some states, history and even science, because there are few state tests in these areas.

Myth 4: One Can Test (Inspect) Quality into Education

The idea that state tests can be ratcheted up by rigorous enforcement that school districts must follow, thus improving quality, embraces several dubious assumptions. Among them are:

- The state test and subsequent variations represent the most appropriate content to be taught, learned, and tested;
- Test content is included in the curriculum content mandated to be taught by the state;
- Sufficient information is available to school system personnel regarding what is going to be tested so that the instructional program can follow the lead of the test;

- The idea that the test represents some epitome of excellence or a sufficient standard in itself and is not merely a minimum or a floor expectation covering the largest possible number of school sites to be affected;
- Sufficient equity within the state's funding formula to enable low-wealth districts the opportunities to comply;
- Sufficient funds for adequate staff development to ensure that as test content shifts, teachers and administrators have ample opportunity to understand the directions and implications in their schools and classrooms.

Our experience in states that are practicing the "test quality into education" idea indicates that they mistake uniformity for quality, that is, consistency is the real goal, as opposed to quality. High-stakes testing can bring about greater consistency in the curriculum to be taught. Indeed, testing is the great homogenizer of curriculum because it forces greater attention to what is tested. But to apply to the greatest number of school districts operating in most states, all testing can do is move glacially over the majority of the districts. What then is the actual definition of quality? The actual definition is that it consists of standards or indices with which the largest number of school systems can comply in the shortest time period. Anything else is simply not politically feasible. Instead of the test being used to determine if quality is present, it is used to define and circumscribe it. This idea is the epitome of the inspection model at work, something Deming's (1986) work punctured with great effect. Deming eschewed improved inspection as the antidote to quality by saying, "Inspection to improve quality is too late, ineffective, costly. . . . Quality comes not from inspection, but from improvement of the production process" (pp. 28–29).

These kinds of tests, which comprise most state tests, are not benchmarks of excellence. Rather, they are benchmarks of minimal adequacy. They can't really be anything else. The unintended effect of hammering school districts with test scores is to flatten the curriculum, reduce diversity, reward minimal performance with commendations, and reduce initiative to engage in reform. In short, the use of standardized tests as accountability tools will standardize the curriculum and everything else. While for some disorganized and corrupt school systems this could be categorized as a change for the better, for the vast majority it is the enshrinement of the bare minimum to shine only in the areas tested. We see this as a loss. We see it as a cudgel against diversity and the Waterloo of local control. That battle is already over; it's history.

THE NATURE OF CURRICULUM ALIGNMENT

There is much to criticize about the testing and accountability movement in the United States. Coffman (1993) highlighted the major concern succinctly: "comparing averages among schools, systems, or states on any test is inherently unfair because it is not possible to separate school effects from effects resulting from nonschool factors" (p. 8). Jensen (1980, p. 724) was even more acerbic when he noted a decade earlier on using test scores to praise or blame schools:

> The public is badly informed by such misguided praise and blame. We have known for years that much of the variation in level of scholastic achievement among schools is predictable from a number of demographic characteristics of the populations they serve. But the schools can have no control over such community characteristics.

Jensen (1980) noted that a school's average I.Q. and achievement scores could be predicted from socioeconomic variables with a multiple correlation "of about 0.60" (p. 724). He cited the work of Thorndike (1951), now almost a half-century old, in knowing the impact of community demographics on achievement test scores.

We have listed some of our concerns and criticisms in this opening chapter. We think that curriculum alignment represents one positive trend that can help school system personnel meet some of the challenges. We note from research literature nearly twenty years old that when the testing content and curriculum content overlapped, such practices were highly significant in explaining improved reading scores. In fact, such overlapping (i.e., alignment) explained 72 percent of the variance of the post-test score gains in one early study by Leinhardt, Zigmond, and Cooley (1981). Later research on the opportunity to learn (OTL) similarly confirmed this study and added such factors as students' attendance rate, content exposure, and quality of instructional delivery as also "significant predictors of students' achievement test scores" (Wang, 1998, p. 150).

Curriculum alignment simply means one teaches children what one tests them on. Although this appears to be common sense, as with the weekly classroom spelling test, it's not so common when applied to a statewide accountability test. Charges that one shouldn't teach to the test are legion. There is much confusion and a large gray area about what constitutes ethical practices. We know of one state where one form of the previous standardized test is freely available and used by school personnel for alignment and in others where such practices are condemned, even if the information is available on the Internet.

That some tests measure nobody's specific curriculum is well known in educational circles. We've been in school systems where we could say, "The schools here are better than their test scores." Although nearly every educator could explain how this could happen (because the test in use doesn't assess the curriculum in use), such an idea is counterintuitive to most educational consumers. The public becomes concerned about low test scores because they believe that the test in use is a valid measure of the *curriculum* in use.

Educators know that tests have been developed apart from any specific curriculum. The standardized tests all reflect a very general notion of what is worth knowing in the subject areas being tested, but the actual overlap to any specific local curriculum may vary greatly. Tests are not neutral tools. Children from cultures that reflect the content found on such tests have an advantage. They come to the tests with the background experiences, the linguistic and conceptual diversity, and greater confidence in their ability to perform on them.

Consider two homes where two children, a boy and a girl, ages ten and eight, are being reared.

In Home A, we have two college-educated adults, a father who is an accountant and a mother who operates her own physical therapy business. The median income is over $200,000 per year. The boy, Edward, is a frequent user of the Internet. His father and he have developed some of their own computer simulations together. The girl, Susan, reads voraciously and loves crossword puzzles. They attend a suburban school that has enriched foreign language in the primary grades. The family takes two to three vacations each year and usually travels to educational places such as museums and art galleries. They have been to three to four foreign countries where they have similarly been immersed in the culture and language of those nations. The children are already talking about the colleges they may attend.

In Home B we find a high school graduate who is working as an assistant manager in a local discount store. His wife is a high school dropout who is a maid at a local motel during peak seasons. Their combined income is $38,000. The son, Ralph, watches a lot of television, mostly cartoons, sitcoms, and sports. The daughter, Margaret, had early problems reading, but with some tutoring after school, is up to grade level. There is little disposable income for anything but the basics in Home B's activities. The vacations they have taken have been brief trips to modest lodging at Las Vegas and did not include anything cultural or remotely educational. The parents do not talk to the children about the opportunities education will provide them. School is something to be endured until one can find a job. There are few books and no computer in the home. The family does not subscribe to a newspaper or any magazines. They buy a copy of *TV Guide* at the supermarket.

Which children are more likely to do better on the state education tests? Although there are always exceptions (Ralph could be a closet Einstein and Margaret could be a Margaret Mead), the probabilities are quite strong that the children from Home A will do much better on standardized and/or criterion-referenced tests than the children from Home B. Edward's use of the Internet and his development of computer simulation games will provide him with applications of numbers and puzzle discernment, and familiarity with conceptual tasks. Susan's reading will give her a wider vocabulary and familiarity with print media and her love of crossword puzzles linguistic and conceptual dexterity as well as practice in concentrating on problem solving, all prized test-taking skills. Their knowledge of art, culture, geography, and attendant vocabularies also enhance their capacity of tackling test problems and even guessing more accurately based on context clues. The cultural capital of Home A is very likely to advantage Edward and Susan over Ralph and Margaret (Bernstein, 1990, pp. 63–93). Wilkins' (2000) research on 1,560 public schools in Virginia showed that cultural capital (defined as percentage of a community served by the school which was white) was a statistically significant factor in predicting passing scores on state achievement tests in math, science, English, and social studies (pp. 8–11).

Edward and Susan come to tests with the kinds of dispositions, knowledge, skills, and backgrounds that will lead to greater schooling success, particularly on tests which are not immediately aligned to any specific curriculum that may have been taught in school. Ralph and Margaret may be just as "smart" natively speaking, but their lack of exposure to the kind of cultural capital encountered on tests will disadvantage them at the outset. Such inequalities are all over the American landscape (Kozol, 1992) and without alignment are simply perpetuated under the mythological testing rubric of fairness, neutrality, and meritocracy when there is nothing of the sort present at all. Without alignment, tests reinforce the inequalities that are already present in the larger society and are reflected in the schools. Tests nail down such inequalities. They result in labels being attached to children based on their income and home conditions, matters over which they have little control. Unaligned tests are those over which school personnel have little to no control. In such circumstances there are no poor schools, there are simply schools serving the poor. Because race and poverty are also interrelated, the socioeconomic fault lines are manifested as racial. One consequence is the persistent black–white achievement gap, which is common throughout the testing and accountability movement (Viadero, 2000). On the other hand, when SES is equalized, one study showed that there was no gap between races on the Graduate Record Exam (Sacks, 1997).

As an educational practice, curriculum alignment is a process in which the curriculum in use is matched to the test in use. By teaching what one is testing, the advantage on unaligned tests, which favors wealth, is depressed or eroded. Children of color and/or poverty can learn as well as any children anywhere. They may require different forms of teaching, skills of application that must be taught directly because they have not been present in print media in the home and are not transferred from home to school, and they must find rewards in the concentration on mental/conceptual puzzles which their previous experience has neither emphasized nor valued.

Tests are part and parcel of the culture in which they are embedded. They could no more be free of that culture than one could be free of certain idiomatic expressions in use in any of the world's languages as one speaks and thinks with those languages. They are of a whole. One of the attributes of culture is that those in it are blind to its impact and use (Hall, 1977). We often overlook how important culture is in forecasting school and test success. That money and test performance are correlated, often expressed in the educational attainment level of the parent (education and income are highly related), should not be used to punish some children while others are rewarded simply because their personal circumstances are more in tune with the tests in use. Above all, we should not succumb to the idea that children who do not score well are in some way genetically or inherently inferior. These are bankrupt notions of the racism and sexism of the last century. We should simply recognize that the tests in use are flawed tools. They value some cultural forms and devalue others. The valuation process is skewed towards those in control of things. The tests reflect what they consider to be most important, which just happens to coincide with what they acquire in their homes and punctuate in their lifestyles. They have more disposable income to purchase a curriculum, which is much more in line with any generic test that could be constructed, including so-called I.Q. or intelligence tests. It is interesting that Alfred Binet, the French creator of the exam that still bears his name, designed his test to assess academic readiness and not any genetic capacity (Fine, 1975, p. 16). What constitutes "academic readiness" is decidedly defined by culture. While it may be conceptually possible to envision intelligence as culture free, it is virtually impossible to construct a test outside a culture. A test is simply a specific type of cultural, human artifact. Stripped of their mystery and jargon, we ought to see tests for what they are: human cultural tools to make decisions about other humans. We ought to be judicious about any application that runs counter to what Americans believe their educational institutions should be.

KEY CONCEPTS OF THIS CHAPTER

Accountability   The idea that "results," however measured, can be traced and connected to those chiefly responsible for their occurrence by their actions or behaviors in context

Cultural capital   The lived experiences and linguistic, conceptual knowledge, skills, and dispositions prized by a specific culture, which are available to be purchased within it by consumers and patrons; and which are also ultimately embedded in schools and the tests in use in schools

Curriculum in use   The actual curriculum being implemented in a classroom, as opposed to the one in the guide, state guide, or state-approved textbook

High-stakes testing   Tests that are highly visible and come with a range of rewards and punishments for doing well or poorly on them

Meritocracy   The idea that social class structure is based on merit irrespective of race, gender, or wealth as measured by some "objective" form of measurement

Opportunity to learn (OTL)   The opportunity for students to learn how to solve a particular problem which will be included on the test(s) in use

Tests in use   A test(s) that is currently being utilized to assess learning or some other characteristic of a classroom or school system

APPLICATIONS

1. Questionnaire to Determine Level of Belief in "Culprits"

Purpose: The purpose of this activity is to determine the degree to which teachers, parents, and community members adhere to the culprits identified in this chapter.

    In order to determine the extent to which the culprits are influencing the thinking of teachers, parents, and community members, develop a simple questionnaire using a Likert scale from zero to five. Ask respondents to indicate to what extent they believe low test scores are the result of each of these culprits. A score of zero could mean "not related," a score of three could mean "somewhat related," and a score of five could mean "definitely related." The instrument could be given to all staff, a random sample of parents, and a random sample of community members. In order to increase the percentage of people responding, the questionnaire could be given out at a district faculty meeting, parent open-house night, and a community event.

The results could be tabulated and printed in the school newsletter. These results could then become part of expanding the dialogue about school accountability.

2. Parent Orientation to District/School Accountability Testing Program

Purpose: The purpose of this activity is to acquaint parents with the design, format, and timing of the present state-mandated testing program.

The district could prepare a workshop designed to acquaint parents and community members with the type(s) of accountability assessments given to students attending the schools. The workshop should be developed by central administration staff and be geared to an audience of parents. Variations of the workshop should be developed for elementary, middle, and high schools. The workshops should be conducted by building-level administrators. Workshop materials should include a general script, all slides (Power Point or similar presentation program) with notes for the speaker, master copies of handouts, and an evaluation form.

The workshop agenda could include the following:

Welcome and introductions   Encourage parents to state their name and respond to this question, "What are your memories about taking state tests in school?" The question is designed to enable parents to talk about both the anxiety-producing aspects of testing and the positive feelings about doing well on tests. Keep this part of the meeting short, but be sure everyone is heard.

Overview of the district's testing program   This should be a K–12 picture of what tests are given at what grade levels and include the content area assessed. For instance, the ITBS may be required at grades three, six, and eight in the areas of mathematics, reading/language arts, and social studies.

Include sample test items if available. Talk about whether the tests are criterion-referenced tests or norm-referenced tests. Explain the difference.

Trends in testing   In this part of the meeting, talk about the trends in testing that are influencing the nature of tests. Many states are incorporating more open-ended response items in tests. Provide the audience with some examples. (The Kentucky Department of Education web site is a good source.) Explain the trends you see that will have an impact on your district/school in the near future.

Analyzing test results   Provide participants with copies of the type of data the district receives back for students, classrooms, schools, and the district. Describe how classroom teachers utilize these data to develop instruction.

General question-and-answer time   End with a general question-and-answer time. The principal may want to invite an assessment specialist to the meeting to help with this part. However, it is important that the building principal be the primary presenter. In this way, parents come to understand the principal's role as instructional leader.

3. Reflective Study Group

Purpose: The purpose of this activity is to engage in reflective thought about the concept of cultural capital in an environment designed to encourage discussion and introspection.

Announce that there will be an opportunity for teachers to join a voluntary study group dealing with the topic of cultural capital. The group will meet for four sessions on a set night for a two-hour period. The time can be set for immediately after school or later in the evening. All materials will be provided for the group (plus snacks). A teacher will lead the discussion. Participants will be asked to read chapters in a selected book before coming to the discussion session (books will be provided by the district). The discussion leader should develop reflective questions to guide the group discussion. Participants will be asked to write a one-page reflective piece about how the experience of meeting and discussing the book affected their thinking about their job and how they may change classroom practices based on the experience.

NOTE: Classroom teachers could seek out opportunities to engage in meaningful dialogue about their profession. Providing these opportunities for teachers is an indication that the school's administration recognizes this valuable practice as a necessary component for teacher growth.

Suggested Books

- *The Right to Learn: A Blueprint for Creating Schools That Work,* Linda Darling-Hammond, San Francisco: Jossey-Bass, 1997.
- *Developing Teachers: The Challenges of Lifelong Learning,* Christopher Day, Philadelphia: Falmer Press, 1999.

- *Teaching to Change the World,* Jeannie Oakes and Martin Lipton, Boston: McGraw Hill, 1999.
- *Justice and Caring: The Search for Common Ground in Education,* Michael Katz, Nel Noddings, and Kenneth Strike, New York: Teachers College Press, 1999.
- *The Schools Our Children Deserve,* Alfie Kohn, Boston: Houghton Mifflin, 1999.

REFERENCES

Apple, M. (1979). *Ideology and curriculum.* London: Routledge & Kegan Paul.

Baker, D. (1993, April). Compared to Japan, the U.S. is a low achiever . . . really. *Educational Researcher* 22 (3), 18–20.

Berliner, D., and Biddle, B. (1995). *The manufactured crisis: Myths, fraud, and the attack on America's public schools.* New York: Longman.

Bernstein, B. (1990). *The structuring of pedagogic discourse: Vol. 4, class, codes, and control.* London: Routledge.

Blau, P., and Scott, W. (1962). *Formal organizations.* San Francisco, CA: Chandler Publishing.

Boyd, J. (1997). Update on SAT scores for 1996–97 school year. Memo to E. Dean, Lake Forest School District, Felton, DE.

Braun, R. (1972). *Teachers and power: The story of the American Federation of Teachers.* New York: Simon & Schuster.

Campbell, G. (1998, March 19). Bridging the gap that divides America. Black Issues in *Higher Education* 120.

Carnoy, M. (1999). Globalization and educational reform: What planners need to know. Paris, France: UNESCO, International Institute for Educational Planning.

Carnoy, M., and Torres, C. (1989). Educational reform and social transformation in Cuba, 1959–1989. In Carnoy, M., and Samoff, J. (eds.) *Education and social transition in the third world,* 153–208. Princeton, NJ: Princeton University Press.

Carnoy, M., and Werthein, J. (1980). *Cuba: Cambio económico y reforma educativa* (1955–1978). Mexico: Editorial Nueva Imagen.

Coffman, W. (1993). A king over Egypt, which knew not Joseph. *Educational Measurement: Issues and Practice* 12 (2), 5–8.

Darling-Hammond, L. (1997). *The right to learn: A blueprint for creating schools that work.* San Francisco: Jossey-Bass.

DelFattore, J. (1992). *What Johnny shouldn't read: Textbook censorship in America.* New Haven, CT: Yale University Press.

Deming, W. (1986). *Out of the crisis.* Cambridge, MA: MIT Press.

Fine, B. (1975). *The stranglehold of the I.Q.* New York: Doubleday.

Finn, C. (1991). *We must take charge.* New York: Free Press.

Gigot, P. (2000, September 1). How—and how not—to fight for vouchers. *The Wall Street Journal,* A10.

Giroux, H. (1997). *Pedagogy and the politics of hope.* Boulder, CO: Westview.

Giroux, H. (1994, October). The challenge of cultural studies to colleges of education. *International Journal of Educational Reform* 3(4), 464–469.

Giroux, H. (1988). *Schooling and the struggle for public life: Critical pedagogy in the modern age.* Minneapolis: University of Minnesota Press.

Glass, T. (1992). *The study of the American school superintendency.* Arlington, VA: American Association of School Administrators.

Gould, S. (1981). *The mismeasure of man.* New York: Norton.

Hall, E. (1977). *Beyond culture.* New York: Anchor Books.

Hernstein, R., and Murray, C. (1994). *The bell curve.* New York: Free Press.

Holt, J. (1998, June 2). The smart set. *The Wall Street Journal,* A20.

Jencks, C., and Phillips, M. (eds.). (1998). *The black–white test score gap.* Washington, DC: Brookings.

Jensen, A. (1998). *The g factor: The science of mental ability.* Greenwood, CT: Praeger.

Jensen, A. (1980). *Bias in mental testing.* New York: Free Press.

Johnston, R. (2000, May 17). Pa. targets 11 districts for takeover: Most will get 3 years to raise test scores. *Education Week* 19 (36) 1, 26.

Johnston, R., and Sandham, J. (1999, April 14). States increasingly flexing their policy muscle. *Education Week* 18 (31), 1, 19.

Kincheloe, J. (1999). *How do we tell the workers? The socioeconomic foundations of work and vocational education.* Boulder, CO: Westview.

Kozol, J. (1992). *Savage inequalities: Children in America's schools.* New York: Harper-Collins.

Kuhn, T. (1962). *The structure of scientific revolutions.* Chicago: University of Chicago Press.

Lehman, N. (1999). *The big test.* New York: Farrar, Straus & Giroux.

Leinhardt, G., Zigmond, N., and Cooley, W. (1981). Reading instruction and its effects. *American Education Research Journal* 18 (3), 343–361.

Lieberman, M. (1960). *The future of public education.* Chicago: University of Chicago Press.

Lieberman, M. (1993). *Public education: An autopsy.* Cambridge, MA: Harvard University Press.

Lieberman, M. (1997). *The teacher unions.* New York: Free Press.

Linn, R. (2000, March). Assessments and accountability. *Educational Researcher 29* (2), 4–16.

Macedo, D. (1994). *Literacies of power: What Americans are not allowed to know.* Boulder, CO: Westview.

McDonald, J. (2000, January). Forty years after the revolution: A look at education reform in Cuba. *International Journal of Educational Reform* 9 (1), 44–49.

McGinn, D. (1999, September 6). The big score. *Newsweek,* 47–51.

Messerli, J. (1972). *Horace Mann: A biography.* New York: Knopf.

Nash, G., Crabtree, C., and Dunn, R. (1997). *History on trial: Culture wars and the teaching of the past.* New York: Knopf.

National Commission on Testing and Public Policy. (1990). *Reforming assessment: From gatekeepers to gateway to education.* Chestnut Hill, MA: Boston College.

Nisbett, R. (1998). Race, genetics, and IQ. In C. Jencks and M. Phillips (eds.) *The black–white test score gap.* Washington, DC: Brookings, 86–102.

Paris, S., Lawton, T., Turner, J., and Roth, J. (1991, June–July). A developmental perspective on standardized achievement testing. *Educational Researcher 20* (5), 12–20.

Portes, P. (1999, Fall). Social and psychological factors in the academic achievement of children of immigrants: A cultural history puzzle. *American Education Research Journal 36* (3), 489–507.

Reich, R. (2000, September 6). The case for 'progressive' vouchers. *The Wall Street Journal,* A26.

Robinson, G., and Brandon, D. (1994). *NAEP test scores: Should they be used to compare and rank state educational quality?* Reston, VA: Educational Research Service.

Sacks, P. (1997, March/April). Standardized testing: Meritocracy's crooked yardstick. *Change,* 25–28.

Stahler (1999, September 6). Cartoon in the Denver *Rocky Mountain News,* 63A.

Stedman, L. (1994, October). Incomplete explanations: The case of U.S. performance in the international assessments of education. *Educational Researcher 23* (7), 24–32.

Steinberg, J. (2000, September 3). Nation's schools struggling to find enough principals. *New York Times,* 1, 16.

Thorndike, R. (1951). Community variables as predictors of intelligence and academic achievement. *Journal of Educational Psychology* 42, 321–338.

Viadero, D. (2000, March 22). Lags in minority achievement defy traditional explanations. *Education Week* 19 (28), 1, 18–22.

Viadero, D., and Johnston, R. (2000, April 5). Lifting minority achievement: Complex answers. *Education Week* 19 (30), 1, 14.

Wald, K. (1978). *Children of Che: Childcare and education in Cuba.* Palo Alto, CA: Ramparts Press.

Wang, J. (1998, Fall). Opportunity to learn: The impacts and policy implications. *Educational Evaluation and Policy Analysis* 20 (3), 137–156.

Wilkins, J. (2000, April). Characteristics of demographic structures and their relationship to school-level achievement: The case of Virginia's standards of learning. Unpublished paper, American Education Research Association, New Orleans, LA.

World Bank (1995). *Strategies for education.* Washington, DC: World Bank.

· 2 ·

Understanding the Dynamics
of the Playing Field

$\mathscr{T}$ he basic construct for curriculum alignment is to ensure that what is tested is what is taught. The idea is that the advantages enjoyed by children from high-wealth circumstances on high-stakes tests of accountability should not unduly privilege them in the process. More importantly, children of poverty and of color are not to be punished for being who they are and from the socioeconomic conditions in which they are enmeshed, in a society in which the gap between the *haves* and *have nots* has been accelerating (Ford and Barta, 2000; Milken, 2000).

For example, an analysis done by the Center on Budget and Policy Priorities, a nonprofit organization based in Washington, D.C., showed that the gap between the rich and poor in America has eroded into a chasm in which "the richest 2.7 million Americans, the top 1 percent, will have as many after-tax dollars to spend as the bottom 100 million" (Johnston, 1999, p.14y). The same data showed that this ratio has more than doubled since 1977, when the top one percent had only as much after-tax money as the bottom 49 million Americans. The Center's provocative findings also indicate that poorer Americans have less wealth today. In real terms, "four out of five households, or about 217 million people, are taking home a thinner slice of the economic pie than in 1977" (Johnston, 1999, p. 14y). About one-fifth of American households (estimated at 54 million people) expanded their share of the national wealth, but more than 90 percent of that gain went to only 1 percent of the households—of which the after-tax income averaged $515,600, up from $234,700 in 1977. By contrast, the poorer one-fifth of American households averaged $8,800 of after-tax income, down from $10,000 in 1977.

Engaging in curriculum alignment does not hold anyone back. It does, however, ensure that the cultural capital loaded into high-stakes tests of accountability is made accessible to everyone through a curriculum in use that is matched to the test in use. This is doubly important for low-income children, since the only place they are likely to encounter the kinds of cultural capital on the tests in use is in school. Low-income children cannot depend on the home to include forms of cultural capital that are likely to be included on tests. The net disposable income available for cultural capital in low-income or poverty homes may be marginal or nonexistent. Even if access to public museums, galleries, and libraries may be free, the education level of the parent may not include a value disposition that understands or takes advantage of them. Such a value disposition does not recognize the importance of such experiences to real world work access. This lack of interest might be incorrectly interpreted as "inability or lack of intelligence" (Kincheloe, 1999, p. 245). More important is the vocabulary/conceptual schemata at work through various forms of culture in which the artifacts displayed in museums and galleries are situated and the extent to which these are part of the working mental machinery/vocabulary of the developing child.

Simply exposing a child of poverty to Picasso won't do much for him/her until and unless the much larger conceptual/artistic/cultural field at work is perceived and utilized. We should add that no culture is "deprived" of anything. Cultures are different. If individuals from one culture dominate the decision-making process at work in determining both curriculum and the tests that ostensibly are aligned to it, the dissonance between cultures can affect how well a child will do on these tests.

For example, Meyers and Rust (2000) recount how a cultural mismatch involving the speaking and listening standards in New York had placed her Chinese students at a disadvantage. The standards called for students to learn how to participate in group conversations in which their voiced opinions conflicted with the rest of the group. For thousands of years, Chinese children have been instructed not to talk at mealtimes and not to argue with adults since that is a sign of disrespect. This powerful cultural norm overshadowed Chinese "achievement" based on Western and American cultural norms about learning how to engage in speaking and listening in a different culture (p. 37).

We also recall a story we personally heard in Canada about the Ministry of Education's experience in Quebec while testing the Inuit in the icy regions of the frozen north. A test question asked Inuit children, "When I come to a boulevard stop, I---." Teachers of Inuit children immediately recognized the problem. There are no boulevard stop signs where the Inuit live. When the French Canadian test makers were devising the test, they assumed that all children would have some cultural experience with this ubiquitous aspect of modern life. In selecting this example, they disadvantaged anyone without such experience, namely the Inuit. It never occurred to them that a boulevard stop sign as a cultural artifact would not be familiar to all children. What if the circumstances were reversed? Since the Inuit are allowed by the government to go walrus hunting from time to time because it is part of their cultural/religious/tribal life, suppose all children in Quebec were asked, "When I am going to go walrus hunting, I---." Such a question would immediately advantage the Inuit children and disadvantage anyone else. Are the Inuit people deprived because they don't know what a boulevard stop sign is? Are the rest of the children culturally deprived because they haven't been walrus hunting? We think the answer is *no* on both counts.

We have also overhead comments by some teachers of inner-city children that "they" (referring to poor African American children) will never understand the more subtle nuances of poetry that sometimes appear in reading or on tests of language arts regarding meter and meaning. We wonder if those same teachers ever observed those "incapable" children at recess or lunch times practicing rap routines in unison where speech, sound, and rhythm are indeed subtly nuanced for anyone who cares to listen and observe. It all depends on who is defining poetry and who ultimately decides what kind of poetry is to be tested. Is it Tennyson or Snoop Doggy Dog? Does the poetry selected stem from the late British Empire and the Crimean War, or the streets of Chicago and the war for survival in the daily realities of ghetto life? Which artifacts from whose culture are to be selected and administered to all in the name of fairness, justice, and equality of opportunity? Just as the children of the suburbs would find the lyrics of some of the rappers puzzling, so do children of the inner city find antinomies in Tennyson. Is anyone genetically deficient or inherently inferior for not understanding the other? We think not but we know many parents, legislators, board members, businesspersons, and educators who do. For example, Raymond B. Cattell, one of the leading figures in studies of intelligence in America, wrote that "much of mankind is obsolete" and that the only real future lay in "breeding for brain size." Part of his plan called for the phasing out of "lesser cultures" (Mehler, 1999, p. 28).

Hirsch's (1987) work in cultural literacy identifies what he and some colleagues posit is superior culture. There is no doubt in any of their minds about what is "right" and "true." What is good for them is good for all, even though they understand it disadvantages some children and their parents from doing well in "their" culture unless they are transformed and adopt it as their own. Such matters are not determined democratically. They are decided by forms of political power. High-stakes tests of accountability are one form of the application of that political power in American life.

Those who control mobility in American life (the collective gatekeepers in which the schools are the primary conduit) subscribe to a form of cultural capital they find comfortable and which reinforces their value framework. The language they use, something called *Standard English*, is the lingua franca of transportation and commerce. It is the mark of an "educated person" who is also likely to possess the literary, linguistic, and conceptual skills to be economically transferable in an information-centered society. These persons are of high value in the global marketplace. They have the cultural capital that is of most worth, highly prized in a capitalistic, competitive, consumer-centered, technology-dominated world. Cultures that find these expressions foreign or juxtaposed to other orientations are at a decided disadvantage in a competitive economic battle to survive in a market-driven environment (see also Raspberry, 1999).

THE BASIC CONSTRUCT:
THE CURRICULUM AND THE TEST

A test is a measure of how well a student has learned the curriculum it is supposed to measure. The weekly Friday spelling test and the quiz on the week's classroom work are normally centered on what was taught and supposed to be learned during that time period. In most circumstances, the one matches the other pretty well. If not, students are not bashful (nor are their parents) about protesting the use of tests that do not assess what was taught. Such tests are considered unfair by nearly everyone. Teachers who persistently violate this norm are to be avoided if at all possible. Teaching and testing different curricula in the classroom can be considered an abuse of power.

The weekly classroom quiz may sample the curriculum taught, that is, it may not have questions about all that was taught, but include questions regarding what the teacher considered the most important things taught. Although teachers often urge their students to prepare for the test by studying everything, students usually know what things are considered more important than others by "psyching" the teacher out as to his or her biases regarding what was most important, or by directly asking the teacher what is most likely to turn up on the test. Some teachers may answer in the phrases of probabilities such as, "Well, you should definitely know . . ." and " a question about . . . may well appear somewhere on the quiz." Test-wise students also know that there is a difference in the way the test question is phrased. They soon learn that preparing for a multiple choice test involving broad coverage of a lot of topics and an essay test about some aspects in greater detail require different types of preparation. Recognition requires one kind of mastery, in-depth understanding of interrelationships quite another.

These very same dynamics characterize test development and administration on a large-scale basis for high-stakes tests of accountability. One large area of difference concerns the use of norm-referenced, standardized tests and criterion-referenced tests as high-stakes measures, but before we deal with this important difference, we have to describe the nature of curriculum and testing in the United States.

THE UNITED STATES: ONE NATION—EXCEPT FOR A CURRICULUM

America stands educationally unique against the rest of the world it so dearly believes it "leads." The U.S. is the sole remaining superpower for the time being. While American foreign policy is directed by defining strategic interests, and American military intervention is defined and measured by the nature of whether those interests are advanced or not, no such objectives or curriculum guides American schools. The simple fact is that there is no American curriculum to speak of. There is federal legislation about education; Native Americans who live on the reservation function under a kind of national curriculum administered in the Department of Interior. But if all America were some gigantic classroom, and all fifty states were the students, this would be one without any specific objectives or any approved curriculum. Each "student" decides his or her own curriculum to learn. The teacher tries to shore up this loose confederation by finding commonalities among the fifty "students" when they agree to search for them. Sometimes they do and sometimes they don't.

Each "student" insists on inserting into his own curriculum peculiarities within their own realm. For example, Pennsylvania insists on teaching about Emma Willard; New Jersey about Captain John Berry; and if a principal doesn't plant a tree in South Carolina on Arbor Day, he or she can be fined fifty dollars. Each "student" insists on spending time on the equivalent of the family tree. Somewhere in the elementary grades, a full year is devoted to the history of that state. In a global society, is it worth it to spend a full year on Texas, California, or Vermont history?

Americans are not only oblivious to the idiosyncrasies of their own notions of schooling and how utterly ridiculous they are, but we generally have a shorter school year than the rest of the nations we compete against. That's because we still adhere to the agrarian calendar when children were needed in the field to harvest the corn and watermelons. The Japanese school year is 243 days compared to 180 for the U.S. (Stedman, 1994, p. 29). Although the length of the school year or the amount of instructional time spent on a curricular area is reported by researchers to have little to no bearing on international achievement scores (Stedman, 1994, pp. 29–30), the long summer period when American students are not in school may be a significant culprit in depressing U.S. achievement, especially for low-income/minority students. In a recent review of thirteen prior studies involving 47,994 elementary and middle school students conducted by the universities of Missouri and Tennessee State, low-income students lost ground in reading over the summer while middle-income students did not. That review hypothesized that this discrepancy may be due to the fact that "middle-income students had more access to books over the summer" (Mathews, 2000, p. 29).

The absurdity of this situation is that, in 1989, President George Bush and the governors meeting in Charlottesville, Virginia (Tucker and Codding, 1998, p. 41) declared that America would be "number one" (as measured by international test scores in math and science) by the year 2000. Maybe the public was gulled, but no one who truly understood the nature of curriculum and tests, and the American peculiarity with them, actually believed it would happen. First, a curriculum response is only part of the problem (Stedman, 1994, pp. 27–30) and Americans are unwilling to engage in large-scale social changes outside of schools to deal with the variables that would affect test scores, such as class, language, gender, and minority status (Stedman, 1994, p. 30).

It wasn't that America couldn't be number one if there were a national will to do it and a genuine understanding of the dynamics it would take to make it happen, but like so many other things, Americans believe the world is Burger King—that is, they can have what they want, the way they want it, on demand—the educational equivalent of fast food. If the rest of the world, with national curriculums monitored by national ministries of education, beats the U.S. on test scores, we want what they have without that level of interference. We want our burger without onions.

To return to our analogy of America as one gigantic classroom, we want to beat the test score of some other class in the school (the world) and let each "student" decide what he or she will learn and write their own test to show it. If there's a question about the comparability of each individual student's test, we'll solve that problem by declaration. The "student" simply proclaims his or her curriculum world class without ever having to prove it. Kentucky did just that in their noteworthy educational reform called *KERA* (see Steffy, 1993; Linn, 2000)

Americans want the benefits of a centralized curriculum without having to have one. They want the blessings of an educational system that removes the differences in quality among and between the states (compare Mississippi to New York, for example) without creating the means to enforce it, except as it pertains to certain constitutional matters regarding discrimination, which falls to the executive branch of government. The United States Constitution created a national system of banking, transportation, commerce, justice, and the military with attendant national agencies and institutions to plan, direct, and implement them; education was left under the old Articles of Confederation, where it remains to this day. The only U.S. president to forcefully advocate a national system of education was Thomas Jefferson, who hired a French consultant to design it (De Nemours, 1812/1923).

How does a nation without a national curriculum design a test to measure its schools? This was the issue facing the test makers when first creating what are known as *norm-referenced, standardized tests* today and bear the names known by nearly anyone familiar with them: the Iowa Test of Basic Skills (ITBS), the Stanford Achievement Test (SAT), the California Achievement Test (CAT), the Comprehensive Test of Basic Skills (CTBS), the Metropolitan Achievement Tests, or the TerraNova.

In a nation with a national educational curriculum, a test maker would design a test that included the curriculum content, and that test would become the basis for determining how well the respective schools were doing. Political decisions would inform the test makers of what was to be tested and the establishment of passing scores as well. The objectives of a national ministry of education would include what each citizen was expected to know and do before being allowed to graduate from any institution in the country. Thus, a student in Mississippi would have to have the same score to graduate as a student in New York. The curriculum would be public. There would be no secrets about its content. No one would wonder exactly what could be on the test.

THE GENIUS OF THE NORM-REFERENCED, STANDARDIZED TEST

None of these necessary conditions existed in the U.S. prior to the time test makers devised the familiar, national standardized tests. Joseph Mayer Rice created the first achievement test in the United States in 1895. It was a spelling test administered to 16,000 pupils. This instrument was followed by tests of arithmetic and language (Mehrens and Lehmann, 1969, p. 130). Joseph Mayer Rice "is the acknowledged father of comparative methodology in educational research," notes historian Herbert Kliebard (1986, p. 22). In 1923, the first standardized test battery, the Stanford Achievement Test, was published (Mehrens and Lehmann, 1969, p. 131). Other such test batteries followed suit.

In constructing these test batteries, the problems of a lack of a national curriculum were solved by creating a substitute called the *content domain*. The content domain was the most likely "stuff" that would make up a national curriculum—if there were one. The test was then a sample of the learning of this content in the area to be assessed. Calling the replacement the content domain also sidestepped the issue of creating a de facto national curriculum; no one commissioned the small group of persons who constructed the content domain or had the task of creating a national curriculum; therefore there wasn't one. Popham (1981) criticized the standardized, norm-referenced tests for the lack of data regarding their content validity, and declared that the test makers' technical manuals contained no "evidence regarding the test's validity, reliability, and other psychometric qualities. In almost no instance will one find really first-rate establishment of the content validity of a norm-referenced test" (p. 104).

The second problem, if there were a national curriculum, consisted of determining what constituted a passing score or what mastery might be, and was solved by comparing scores to one another, that is, the students who took the test were compared to themselves. The students themselves became the "norms." To declare the test "national," all that was necessary was to include in the norming procedures a very large sample of respondents from all walks of life. Efforts were made to include children from rural and urban areas, a good mix of ethnic folk, and a balance between males and females. This became the norm-referenced group that became the national benchmark. To say that George Smith scored in the seventieth percentile on the ITBS in fourth-grade math doesn't mean that George has mastered fourth-grade math or even that George has a passing fluency, familiarity, or knowledge of what has been determined to be the national fourth-grade math curriculum because there isn't one! What it means is this: compared to all of the other fourth graders in the norming sample who took this test at the time it was defined, George did better than 69 percent of them, and 29 percent did better than George on the problems he had to solve, which were extrapolated from and represented the content domain defined by those who had previously devised the test (see Yardley, 2000, p. 34).

Furthermore, by assuming that all students would have equal access to this content domain because it would be found about evenly within any local or state curriculum (since it was a product of what was believed to be within most local or state curricula as far as could be determined), the content domain was the equivalent of a random variable (everyone had about the same chance of coming into contact with it), and the scores could be graphed. A student's score was considered a form of a continuous variable, and like height, weight, and intelligence, could be represented as such in the so-called bell curve. Thus, achievement and intelligence are highly correlated (and we would say wealth as well).

The test makers did not have to take into consideration that perhaps a test score on their content domain that was loaded with cultural capital, unevenly distributed within the larger populace, was not random at all. The fact that poverty and race are correlated in America might explain why some minorities and Native Americans on reservations were at the tail of the bell curve. Such a ranking is usually attributed to lack of intelligence because of the high correlation between achievement and I.Q. tests, or as Kincheloe (1999) says, "difference is not deficiency: the poor, not the stupid" (p. 245).

The alleged fairness of norm-referenced, standardized tests rests on the assumption that everyone has about the same chance of learning the content domain. Differences in scores are the result of the presence or absence of learning that has been open and fair (*equal*) to all. If this is true, then those with lower scores didn't learn as well (as demonstrated by the test) and the results could not be due to a nonrandom variable (such as wealth) but may be caused by genetic deficiencies or other inherent inferiorities peculiar to them as human beings. We should note that intelligence, as measured by an intelligence test, was considered to be random, that is, assuming a bell-curve distribution.

If intelligence is randomly distributed in the population as a continuous variable, and access to the content domain was also similarly random, differences in achievement were probably due to differences in native ability. Simply put, the smarter kids got better test scores because they were smarter.

The testing companies even worked out a formula for determining if a child did better than "expected." It involved calculating some measure of intelligence with a measure of learning from the standardized test. If an achievement score was greater than the actual score as measured by intelligence, the child was "exceeding expectations" or "doing better than expected." If the reverse were true, then a smarter kid was performing less than his "ability" indicated in his studies.

Anastasi (1976, p. 402) has criticized this practice as a misuse of tests. She observes that such "intra-individual differences in test scores reflect the universal fact that no two tests (or other performance indicators such as course grades) correlate perfectly with each other." The so-called under or over achievement of a student is more a result of "the underprediction or overprediction from the first to the second test." Anastasi indicates that such errors can be attributed to:

- The lack of reliability of the tests;
- Differences in content coverage;
- Differences in attitudes and motivational effects involved with the two tests;
- Differences in certain interventions, such as remedial teaching and/or a prolonged absence from school.

All of these differences are ignored in the simplistic comparison and calculation from ability to achievement. Some of the folks who subscribe to this type of logic deal with wealth as an explanatory variable by arguing that, over time, smarter kids get richer because they acquire more education. Since education and income are correlated, that explains why richer kids do better on tests than poorer ones. Thus, the cultural capital argument is also naysayed. Richer parents are also smarter parents. They reproduce smarter children who in turn do better in schools because they are smarter. When the data is shown that these differences also follow racial and gender lines, as in the case with African Americans, Hispanics, and women, the same logic is extended, though more softly because it is out-and-out racist and sexist. The continuing support for a racist explanation is based on rejection of the idea that whatever intelligence is (as measured by the tests which are assumed to be culture free or at least culturally neutral and not biased), it is simply not randomly spread out within races or between the sexes, even though by formal testing the "smartest" person in the world is a female journalist named *Marilyn Jarvik* with an I.Q. of 228 (Simonton, 1994, p. 219).

The argument goes something like this: while African Americans may be better tap dancers, NBA basketball players, or jazz musicians, there simply isn't enough mental genetic ability in the overall talent pool to have an equivalent number of nuclear physicists, lawyers, surgeons, or Fortune 500 CEO's comparable to the ratio in the white, male population. The same is assumed to be true for Hispanics and women; at least the so-called factual data are often explained that way. It is worth taking a moment to see that the domination of white males in the United States accounts for the fact that half of the nation's industrial worth belongs to a mere one hundred corporations; 54 percent of the corporate leaders and 42 percent of government leaders graduated from twelve private universities, which historically discriminated against women and have very low numbers of African American and Hispanic students (Heilbrunn, 1996, p. 9). These universities use SAT scores, among a variety of measures, to admit students. The correlation between wealth and SAT scores has already been noted by Sacks (1997, p. 27), who also indicated that in the most selective colleges in the nation, fully one-third of the high scorers came from the upper-income brackets. In contrast, only 8 percent came from the lower levels (Sacks, 1997, p. 27). The explanation for why this is so is not very pretty, fair, objective, or even scientific, and there are many who believe the opposite (see Hernstein and Murray, 1994).

To continue the logic of the argument for the moment, if wealth and cultural capital can be explained away through genetic racism and social Darwinian excuses, then a direct line can be cut to *school* performance as a possible cause of poor *test* performance. Poor teaching and/or mediocre teachers, poor leadership on the part of principals, group resistance to change reinforced by rampant unionism, and the lack of incentives for the "monopolistic" public schools to engage in reform are not considered in this argument. This tenuous line of reasoning, which links test score performance to the simple remedies bandied about in the general media today, is used to advance causes and approaches that would disband the public school system by critics who base their case in whole or in part on poor test scores. Make no mistake about it, the accountability movement has been good for the testing industry. Sacks (1997) notes that between 1960 and 1989 standardized test sales doubled in the U.S. to $100 million a year. At the same time, enrollment in U.S. schools increased only by 15 percent (p. 25). In 1996, Achieve, Inc., a nonprofit group supported by business leaders to support improving student achievement, indicated that the fifty states spent "about $165 million on tests" (Boser, 2000, pp. 1, 22). It is estimated that where eighteen states now require students to pass a test to graduate from high school, that number will have risen to twenty-six states by the year 2003 (Yardley, 2000, p. 33).

The shoals on which the assertion of fairness of norm-referenced, standardized tests (and criterion-referenced tests as well) founders is a documented set of predictors, beginning with the Coleman Report in 1966, that indicated attendance at specific schools has little or nothing to do with predicting test score results. The major predictors were SES (socioeconomic status) variables leading to Coleman's incorrect premise that schools did not make a difference in achievement. Since the sample used by Coleman was extremely large in scope, it presumably included a random population of educational personnel, which would include superior teachers and principals as well as inferior ones. But if there are no statistically significant variables related to school that affected student learning on the tests, how can the tests be used to condemn the curriculum, the teachers, or the principals working in them? If the test results are not predicted by any school-controlled variables, how can they be used as a measure of accountability? One can only be accountable for what one can control.

The matter of the lack of control was underscored in a review by Robinson and Brandon (1994) of the National Assessment of Educational Progress (the NAEP). Robinson and Brandon reported that 89 percent of the variance in state average scores was explained by the combined effects of four demographic factors over which the schools had no control (number of parents living at home, the education of the parents, community type, and the state poverty rate) (p. ii). They concluded that since the NAEP-92 trial state assessment results "were shown not to be valid measures of the relative quality or proficiency of mathematics instruction among the states, [that they] should not be used to compare or rank states according to the quality or proficiency of their educational programs" (p. ii).

A similar review of international test performance by Jaeger (1992) indicated that from one-third to more than one-half of the variations in achievement were explained by poverty rates, divorce rates, the percentage of single-parent homes, and student's job activities. International writing performance results were also influenced by variables in the student, family, and the media (Schick, DeMasi, and Green, 1992).

UNDERSTANDING THE FORCES
THAT COMPRISE THE "PLAYING FIELD"

Those who develop a norm-referenced, standardized test begin by constructing a curriculum, actually known as the content domain of the test.

The content domain represents the total possible playing field upon which the content of the test could be drawn. Thus, the content domain is the conceptual boundary for any test. It separates those possible test questions that could be included and those questions that are simply not appropriate (see figure 2-1).

A content domain may not be a curriculum in the sense that it may not represent a specific knowledge base expected to be taught similarly to every child who might take the test. The content domain is considered representative of a broad array of topics, ideas, concepts, and skills, which from the sources utilized in reaching consensus about it are thought to be typical. If a test is also supposed to function as a diagnostic tool, test developers may put in some items that are beyond the immediate grade level, but may be indicative of advanced learning. This is an important point when considering possible ethical violations in the phrase "teaching to the test."

Norm-referenced, standardized tests may include pieces and parts of any local or state curriculum. Because they represent only a sample of the larger content domain, the idea of solely teaching to that which is included on them substantially narrows the curriculum to what is tested, even if what is included on the test is considered the most important part of that content domain.

It would be the same in a classroom. If the teacher has taught a very wide curriculum, but has time only to examine the students on a fraction of that which was taught, to inform students ahead of time of what is to be

Figure 2.1   Content Domain and Test Forms

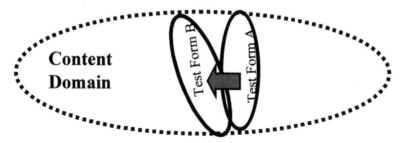

- the content domain is the "curriculum" being assessed, though its actual presence in any specific school is not considered anything but random or else the "bell curve" would be an inappropriate frequency distribution to use by which to "norm" the test results
- various test forms may sample a different part of the content domain or much of the previous form, though with different test items

tested would be to discourage them from studying the whole curriculum, as opposed to only the part that would be tested. Studying for tests is an important part of learning. Preparing for a test is simply another form of teaching and experienced teachers know that they do not want to limit learning by having students study only on what they may tested.

When teachers assign students a grade based on the test results, and they want the test to be a good measure of what students have learned about *all* they taught, to inform students ahead of time of only that fraction of the test that samples their teaching presents a false picture of the total student learning. A judgment about what students actually learned about the whole curriculum would be inaccurate if all students really studied was that parcel of the curriculum tested.

We say that if the teacher wants to make an inference about total student learning based on the test that sampled the entire curriculum, students must study the entire curriculum or the data presented by the test may not be an accurate measure of their learning the whole curriculum. This is not a problem if the test includes everything that was taught and students understand that everything will be tested. Although this might be possible in an individual classroom, it is not possible on high-stakes tests of accountability for an entire state. Testing once at the fourth, eighth, and twelfth grade levels involves a sufficiently wide sweep of the curriculum that there is not enough time to test everything. The test must therefore sample the curriculum. If state education officials want to make an inference about how well students have learned the entire curriculum from the one that was sampled, they cannot afford to inform students, teachers, or parents what part of the curriculum might be included or they compromise the validity of the inference they wish to make regarding the curriculum learned from the one tested. This is one function of keeping the test a secret and insisting on secrecy surrounding exactly what and how the test will be utilized.

The fourth-grade state math test ostensibly represents what a child knows about the entire math curriculum not only at the fourth grade, but earlier grades as well. Yet no test could possibly include all of that which may be included in grades K–4 for math. Teachers must teach the entire curriculum and students must expect to be examined over that curriculum for the test score to have meaning or to represent in some valid way the students' mastery over the K–4 math curriculum. Advanced information that compromises test security compromises the subsequent judgment desired to be made by the state agency itself in dealing with schools and school districts that do not pass muster. Above all else, state agencies want to judge what they believe to be the quality of education in school districts by test scores. Despite the denials often overheard by state officials to avoid undue criticism about overreliance on single and limited measures, nearly everyone—the legislature, the media, the general public, nearly all real estate agents we know, and state officials themselves—form judgments of school systems based on comparable test scores. When the concept of quality can be reduced to a number, something magical appears to happen. Box scores, rankings, "top ten" lists, and other claptrap of an obsession with being "number one" are generated. Newspaper editorials in local media take turns praising or bashing the schools. Since education is one of the largest single consumers of tax funds, the schools are singled out and crude cost comparisons between inputs and outputs described.

Some states like Texas and Florida have devised a categorical ranking system for schools. These roughly correspond to a kind of grading system where "A" schools are "exemplary" and "D" schools are "below average." Enormous pressure is exerted to "improve"—which means moving up in the categorical rankings (see Mintz, 2000). That nearly always and exclusively means doing better as measured by test scores, the common denominator at work, and the impact on educators in the schools is rarely considered. If the idea that the schools can be improved by testing quality (a notion we dispute), then this answer by a high school principal in Texas is apocryphal. When asked if his school was "exemplary," he replied, "No, but we're three students and two test items away from it." People who want schools to be driven by tests in order "to improve them" should ponder the response of this principal. Do we really want tests to become the be-all and end-all of education? Do we really want baseline measures to be indicators of quality? Do we really believe that the tests are the hallmark of an educated individual? Where does the curriculum fit in to this equation? Shouldn't we be concerned about the entire curriculum being taught and not simply that part of it that is tested?

We've also observed procedures that have led to teaching practices that result in incredible student boredom. Some principals and teachers, frightened that they will be found wanting in their state's accountability scheme, have resorted to taking the publicly released test items, extrapolating the skills from them, placing them on ditto sheets, and using them to drill students. This "drill and kill" approach is the equivalent of arsenic in the education well. It not only destroys any kind of creative teaching, it reduces learners to automatons. We've seen too many classrooms in too many states where this kind of "instructional lobotomization" has occurred. It is deadly and destructive on the human spirit. It turns schools into psychological morgues for the early brain-dead (see Mintz, 2000, p. 7).

THE FALLACY OF "VALUE-ADDED" MEASURES

The notion of "value-added" test score gains is a wrinkle in the idea of pay for results, which has a long history in America and England (Madaus and Kellaghan, 1992, p. 122). The new wrinkle is that such results represent the value-added nugget to the pay-for-results idea. Some states like Tennessee (Sanders and Horn, 1994) and Georgia (Archer, 2000b) have instituted the notion of value-added education using tests as benchmarks. The gist of the idea is to assess initially and then again after a period of teaching. Teachers get paid by what they "added" to learning from the initial assessment. One alleged advantage of this concept is that the wealthier school systems, whose children have many advantages, will always score higher and receive accolades they may not deserve in many state testing programs; they may be simply coasting on the higher socioeconomic status of the children who attend their schools. In the value-added scheme, even for these children, one would expect advancement on the test. So if there are no gains, no pay enhancement occurs.

We think this idea is terribly flawed because it is based on the assumptions that all children have equal access to test content (see Jensen, 1980, p. 716), that the effects of cultural capital can be neutralized, and that the test is sufficiently internally homogenous to permit a fair relationship between points gained on test scales to pay adjustments. Is a gain at the high end of the psychometric scale as easily attained as at the low end of the scale? Does it take the same energy and professionalism to go from 51 percent correct to 60 percent as from 91 percent to 100 percent? We think not. "Value-added" schemes assume test homogeneity (that is, all of the problems within the test are of the same level of difficulty) when there is abundant evidence that this condition is not so, especially on norm-referenced tests where the more difficult problems come at the end of the exam. For example, suppose an eighth-grade math test is comprised of 40 percent percentage problems of all kinds. About 5 percent of the remaining questions pertain to solving algebraic equations. Another 5 percent pertain to elementary statistical analysis. The teacher who wants to be paid more and has a class that has not mastered percentage has a different task from the teacher who has a class that has mastered percentage but not algebraic equations. These problems are of a different magnitude. While some psychometric scaling eliminates the problem by employing ratio/interval assumptions (that is, that all items are of the same difficulty and magnitude), the actual operational difficulty in the classroom belies that assumption. Test scaling simply eliminates the instructional problem, but for the teacher such assumptions are absurd. Depending on the subject matter being taught, it may be far easier to move a class from 51 percent to 60 percent than from 91 percent to 100 percent in eighth-grade math or any other area tested. We think the opposition to paying teachers by test scores is appropriate given the false assumptions involved in the tests themselves (see Archer, 2000a, p. 5). Furthermore, we note that the idea is rejected by accountability experts who advise, "Don't put all of the weight on a single-test" (Linn, 2000, p. 15). Even officials of the testing companies, such as Michael Kean, the vice president of public and governmental relations at CTB McGraw-Hill, has publicly said, "High-stakes decisions should not be made on a single measure" (Boser, 2000, p. 22).

The advice about not placing all of the decisions on one measure is both psychometric and practical. Psychometrically, the test makers understand better than anyone else the inherent limitations of their products, and the fact that any test is a very limited measure of that which it purports to assess. Practically, simple scoring errors can have an enormously negative impact when they involve such solitary measures. For example, in St. Paul, Minnesota, 336 high school seniors were denied graduation because of incorrect grading of a math test. Nearly 8,000 students were told they had failed the state test when they had actually passed it. Minnesota Education Commissioner Christine Jax said, "I am outraged by the errors committed by NCS and the harm they have caused Minnesota students, families, and schools" (Associated Press, July 30, 2000, p. A13). The testing company offered a $1,000 tuition aid to any student who had been denied entrance to college based on faulty scoring.

We agree with the following summary of pay for results by Madaus and Kellaghan (1992, p. 121).

> Much of the testing . . . today (particularly mandated, high-stakes testing), its sponsorship, financial base, character, and use, is . . . essentially bureaucratic and only secondarily educational.

Carnoy (1999, p. 68) puts the matter this way: "for testing to have a significant effect on student performance . . . it has to be part of a more systematic effort to assist teachers (and schools) to improve classroom practice."

When the purpose of testing is not to create a means to review what students have learned and reteach if necessary, but solely as a salary mechanism, we think testing has been corrupted. Tests are no longer the means to help individual students or to engage in inferences about programs or curricula (see Madaus and Kellaghan, 1992, p. 135). Group gains are all that matter. Whatever positive information that would be useful for teachers to assist individual students, or for school administrators to understand curricular or programmatic deficits, is lost. Such pay-for-results schemes are political exercises of power.

THE "TEACHING TO THE TEST" CONUNDRUM: WHAT IS ETHICAL?

The accusation of "teaching to the test" is one of the most ubiquitous criticisms about the practice of curriculum alignment. Many members of the general public, and even some educators, don't really understand what teaching to the test actually entails (Raspberry, 1999, p. A8). In fact, the phrase is so general as to require further elaboration (Popham, 2000).

Consider for the moment the weekly classroom spelling test as an example. The traditional procedure is to introduce on Monday the twenty-five words to be spelled correctly on Friday of the same week. Students study the same twenty-five words all week. They take a practice test on Wednesday, which is likely to be the same form of the test to be used on Friday. When Friday comes, the teacher quizzes the class on the same twenty-five words in exactly the same way (form) as they have been practicing all week. Thousands of teachers teach spelling this way, week in and week out. Is this a violation of some code of ethics of testing? If it is, thousands of teachers are unaware of it and the spelling book publishers are likely as ignorant.

Consider the violations of some notions of good teaching and testing practices at work in this example (see Miyasaka, 2000):

- A teacher should not focus instruction solely on the content to be tested because it may produce "inflated scores," and
- A teacher should not practice on the current form of the test.

In the first instance, such a practice is considered inappropriate; in the second instance, the practice is considered unethical (Miyasaka, 2000, p. 6).

It is clear that the weekly spelling test does violate these rules set forth by Miyasaka (2000). Why then is it not considered either inappropriate or unethical as she describes in her AERA paper?

Let us change the situation to reflect current practices in other subject matters. Suppose on the weekly spelling test the teacher decides to have students study the twenty-five words, but she is only going to test them on five (one-fifth) of them. She will use the test score from the five to represent how well the students know the remaining twenty words. In this circumstance, the weekly spelling test is a sample of the larger content domain.

If the teacher teaches only the five words that she knows will be on the test from the list of twenty-five to the students, she cannot use the results to infer accurately that they indeed know the remaining twenty words just as well. She will have only taught to the test instead of teaching the entire content domain, that is, all of the twenty-five words. Because she taught only the five words on the test, her efforts will improve student results, but only for the five words and not for the remaining twenty words. Thus, her efforts produced inflated results because the scores would be better than the students would have done if they had been tested on all of the twenty-five words, or even another five chosen from the remaining twenty words.

If the teacher is going to use the results to certify to the principal, parents, or the state education agency that her students could spell all of the twenty-five words at the same level of accuracy, her statement of the results would be fraudulent. In this sense, the portrayal of those results would be unethical.

Some states have become overzealous in their efforts to stigmatize as unethical those efforts that have been used to improve scores on mostly norm-referenced, standardized tests. We know of at least one state that adopted a popular norm-referenced test because it was the cheapest one they could purchase. The state legislature then passed a law making the use of the norm-referenced test mandatory. The scores from this test are flashed across the state and end up on the front pages of virtually every newspaper in the state when they are released. Local school superintendents are fearful that they might lose their jobs because they were unable to show improvement on this test.

Although the state created its own curriculum, the norm-referenced, standardized test is not aligned (matched) to that curriculum. The extent to which it is a fair measure of the state's actual curriculum is unknown, nor is it aligned to any textbook that would be used by any teacher in the state.

Teachers are hired to teach a curriculum and not a test. When the correlation or match (alignment) is ambiguous to the curriculum teachers have been hired to teach, the teachers have no way of knowing if their work will result in improvements on the test. When they end up using old test items, which are like the ones actually used, "they think they have no alternative. More often than not, those teachers are correct" (Popham, 2000, p. 8). Popham goes one step further by declaring, "Any test that is apt to induce instructional pressures on teachers must either provide clarified descriptions of the content it assesses or it should not be employed" (p. 8).

We know that in Idaho teachers and administrators are forbidden to use old test items from the norm-referenced test in use, even though they could legally obtain previous versions in neighboring states or even from the test publisher. One principal who did so lost her job, though she did not lose her license. In another state, old test items on the same norm-referenced test used in Idaho are freely available to school personnel, a practice authorized by the state department of education as acceptable.

Test corruption refers to any practices whose use would weaken the inferences education agencies want to make from the test scores. Such "corruption" is widespread because of incorrect usage (see Haladyna, Nolen, and Haas, 1991; Hoff, 2000, pp. 1–14) as well as simple out and out cheating, which is a more blatant and obvious violation of instructional practice (see Johnston and Galley, 1999, p. 3).

The matter of ethical behavior as it pertains to "correct" use of the test in relation to a curriculum is at least partly concerned with what kind of inferences one desires to make based on the educational/instructional situation at hand. If the test is a sample of the larger curriculum, and one desires to generalize about the learning of the larger curriculum from the sample, great care must be taken not to pollute the rigor of the inference based on practices that would comprise that generalization.

On the other hand, if the entire curriculum is to be tested because it was also taught, and format variance is not an issue (that is, only one format will be used as in the case of the weekly spelling test), one not only teaches to the test, one teaches the test because the curriculum (content domain) and the test are identical.

Over seventy years ago, John Dewey (1928) characterized schools that were traditional as embracing test scores and I.Q. tests as a way of becoming "better" (meaning efficient). Such attempts would only be appropriate if we believed, he said, that "we are satisfied upon the whole with the aims and processes of existing society" (Kliebard, 1986, p. 192). Here we have a theme of social justice in action, a theme we will take up again in chapter 5. Tests that only make schools more efficient (cheaper) will not redress socioeconomic inequities. Without that, schools perpetuate a problem rather than become a solution to it.

We think that the tests in use perpetuate this problem. We agree with Jensen (1980) when he said, "tests are not simply to be regarded as good *in principle*. They are good only to the extent that they can serve useful and beneficial purposes and can do so more objectively, reliably, and efficiently than other available means" (p. 736). However, we disagree with

Jensen when he portrays psychological tests, and this includes nearly all tests including achievement tests, as objective. Achievement and intelligence tests are measuring culturally imbued and situated knowledge in a social context that is not neutral. Although the tests themselves may be objective calibrations, that which defines them is not. Culture is not objective, it simply exists. There are cultural differences. Culture exists in a power structure, that is, it is politically situated, and dominant cultures are repressive to other cultures. Jensen (1980) decries blaming the testing industry because they can't explain the differences that the tests they sell reveal. Jensen believes that one should assume an "agnostic stance"(p. 737) on tests until science can explain the causes of the differences the tests demonstrate. What Jensen does not grasp is that the science itself, and its pre-assumptions about the objectivity of that which it is assessing, conceals the causes in its own worldview (Usher and Edwards, 1996, pp. 33–55). To assume an agnostic stance assures that the so-called causes will remain hidden. Science is nothing more than a series of habits and its objectivity is a myth.

> Western reason is not transparent to itself, as it loves to believe, but actually founds itself on a constitutive blind spot; its willful refusal to recognize the others it dominates. This dominated other (in a master-slave dialectic) is both within the system and invisible. (McGowan, 1991, p. 102)

In the next several chapters, we develop an approach to improving tests scores for all children on high-stakes accountability measures. However, we are most concerned with those children who are culturally different—not deficient. These are generally the children of the poor and also largely children of color. We do not believe they should be punished, demeaned, or ridiculed as less capable because of their cultural differences. The steps we demonstrate in the idea of curriculum alignment have a long history in the literature, as some of our citations reveal.

The ultimate challenge is to change the testing practices in education, to recognize that all tests are assessing culture, and to acknowledge that schemes to punish and reward students, teachers, and administrators because of their cultural proclivities represent political agendas and are expressions of political power. There is nothing scientific or neutral about the manifestations of those agendas, but such recognition will be a long time coming. Meanwhile there are children, teachers, and administrators in the existing system who matter and who care. We believe that the system as it now functions can and must be made fairer, and we show how this can be accomplished.

KEY CONCEPTS OF THIS CHAPTER

Curriculum alignment   A match between the written, taught, and tested curricula. Sometimes referred to in the literature as "curriculum overlap" between the curriculum content and the tested content. Alignment raises the probability that the written curriculum will be learned because it will be taught.

Content domain   The curriculum that becomes the basis for inclusion on a test. The "sample" for a test is taken from this larger content domain, the largest possible "pool" from which test items could be developed.

Criterion-referenced tests   Tests that are referenced to specific objectives and student responses, provided in proportion to the number answered correctly or incorrectly

National curriculum   The curriculum of a nation–state; for the United States, a potential curriculum would represent what the "average American" should know.

Norm-referenced test   A test scored by indicating how an individual student did compared to all the others who took the same test. Reporting scores by percentiles is a typical method of data presentation of norm-referenced tests.

Objective   The antonym of subjective; an assumption that a practice has no bias that would skew effort or results more in one direction than another, and that the differences obtained (variance) would not result from such biases being present. A highly disputed concept within research and educational practice today.

Teaching to the test   A generic phrase, most often used as a criticism, of paying too much attention to a test and simply teaching the current test in use, which can be unethical. However, the phrase can also mean teaching to the objectives or to the content of the test, which are not unethical practices.

Test ethics   Lawful or regulative practices that pertain to teaching and testing, usually established to protect the integrity (security or secrecy) of the tests in use

Value-added   The idea that the monetary value of a practice, procedure, or service in a work organization can be connected to the individual worker or work unit based on measurement before and after the work has been performed

APPLICATIONS

1. A Survey of Childhood Experiences

Purpose: The purpose of this activity is to gain an understanding of the experiences children have had prior to entering school to gauge the degree of cultural capital children bring to the learning experience.

This is an activity that should be completed by parents during the routine kindergarten orientation. It could be administered orally if there is sufficient teacher time to engage in this type of conversation with a parent or a primary caregiver. If time will not permit the oral conversation, then a questionnaire could be developed to solicit the information. It is extremely important that the questionnaire be constructed in a way that is nonthreatening to the parent providing the information. Inserting questions regarding travel, books, reading time, conversation, and types of television programs typically watched can be infused with questions regarding number of siblings, access to extended family, pets, favorite sports, and best friends.

An interesting application of this survey would be to ask the question of the person admitting the student to school and also ask the questions, separately, of the student. Noting the similarities and differences in the responses can provide educators with valuable insight into the learning environment of the home.

2. Analyzing Tests in Use to Determine Cultural Context

Purpose: The purpose of this activity is to become aware of the cultural context embedded in the current test in use in the district/school.

Obtain copies of publicly released tests or portions of tests currently used as accountability measures by the state. Review test items to determine the level of cultural literacy embedded in the questions. For instance, a chart depicting different types of tennis shoes to be used for different purposes such as running, cross training, basketball, track, and leisure assumes that the reader is aware of these different types of shoes. Lack of this knowledge may interfere with a student's ability to demonstrate his/her understanding of how to read the chart and answer the questions correctly. A question about the impact of coal mining on the local economy may have completely different meaning for a fourth grader in eastern Kentucky; one living in Santa Fe, New Mexico; and one living in Harlem, New York.

By examining the tests in use for cultural context, it is possible to determine the match between children taking these tests and the cultural context knowledge required to do well on the tests. Where there are discrepancies, this information can be shared with teachers. Teachers can then design instructional sequences to make students more aware of these contexts.

3. Determining How High-Stakes Tests Were Developed or Selected

Purpose: The purpose of this activity is to gain an understanding of how high-stakes tests were selected and/or developed in your state.

The adoption of high-stakes tests as state accountability measures always involves action by the state legislature. Gaining an understanding of the events that lead to this adoption in your state can provide educators with valuable information about the beliefs and attitudes of state officials, business leaders, and the general public. It can also lead to the identification of the influential stakeholders in the process.

Every school administrator needs to spend some time getting to know how the state legislature works, particularly the legislative education committee. It is time well spent to attend some committee meetings when the general assembly is in session. It is just as important to listen to the dialogue as it is to take note of who is in attendance at these meetings. When the education subcommittee is meeting, there are almost always representatives from major professional groups such as the teachers' associations, school administrators, parent organizations, and school board associations. A large contingent of state department officials is usually present; many times they will be testifying before the committee. Members of the press assigned to cover education news are also present. Whether this includes television coverage is usually dependent upon the issues being discussed.

Also present are several representatives from the legislative support group, sometimes called the Legislative Research Commission. These are individuals who work for the legislature and are generally involved in conducting background literature reviews, drafting legislation, and keeping in touch with what other state legislatures are doing. Developing a casual professional relationship with these individuals keeps you in touch with the legislative trends that often result in statutes.

Long before legislation is passed, the education subcommittee hears testimony from a variety of stakeholders on any given topic. This testimony is recorded and becomes part of the official historical record, so it is often possible to trace the development of legislation by reading the minutes of these meetings. It is usually fairly easy to guess the position a legislator will take by reviewing the type of questions asked during these meetings.

If it isn't possible to attend these hearings, the state administrator organization usually has a summary of these meetings on their web site. It should be mandatory reading for all school administrators. The best time to influence legislation is when it is being developed. If legislation under consideration in not in the best interests of children, it is possible to mount an information campaign that can change the course of the development of the statute.

At the very least, school administrators should actively involve local legislators in dialogue about the impact of legislation. Politicians want to believe that the laws they pass have a positive impact on public education. Providing them with firsthand evidence that this is true, and making suggestions for further improvements, should be part of the job description of every administrator.

It is our belief that this is an area where current school administrators are deficient. The Interstate School Leaders Licensure Consortium (ISLLC) standards include the responsibility of every school administrator to exert influence to improve public education. Activity in the political arena speaks to this important standard.

4. Determining Loss of Learning over the Summer

Design and conduct an action research study to document the loss of learning experienced by students in your district over the summer. This study could be conducted at the elementary or middle school level. Identify a group of students who are receiving instruction throughout the summer and another group (randomly selected, if possible) who did not participate in summer school. The population for the study could be students falling below the fortieth percentile in reading, as measured by the state accountability test administered in the spring of fourth grade. Because summer school attendance is not mandatory, it should be possible to identify students who went to summer school and those who did not. Compare the achievement of students in the fall using a parallel form of the test. You could also compare attendance rates, grades, and attitudes of these two groups of students. The results could be used to stimulate discussion regarding a variety of subjects, including year-round schools and other programs that could be offered in the summer.

5. Surveying Teachers about Testing Practices

Most teachers use the same type of teacher-made tests throughout the school year. It is informative to determine some basic information about the tests teachers employ. A short questionnaire could be developed that asks teachers for the following information.

- How often do you administer tests?
- Approximately how long does the test take?
- What format is used for test items? If multiple forms are used, specify the percentage of questions for each format.
- What feedback is provided to students regarding test results?
- How are students provided with both formative and summative feedback regarding their progress?

The results of this type of survey can be used to compare the testing environment of the classroom with the testing environment of the accountability assessment. For example, if English teachers at the secondary level consistently use essay questions and the state assessment is a multiple-choice test, students may not be accustomed to the context of the state assessment, and this alone may impede their ability to do well on the state test.

These survey results can also be used to discuss the nature of assessment and the value of using a variety of assessment formats as part of the teacher's repertoire.

6. Conducting Focus Groups Dealing with "Teaching to the Test"

Purpose: The purpose of this activity is to enable teachers to have a dialogue about the meaning of the concept "teaching to the test."

The idea of teaching to the test has a variety of meanings for educators. Some view it as an inappropriate activity. Others believe it is unethical. Still others believe it is good educational practice. It is important for administrators to understand how teachers view this concept. This is an activity where the district might want to contract with an outside agent to conduct these focus groups and prepare a written summary of the findings. If there is a local college in the area, a faculty member may be interested in this work. Teachers invited to attend the focus groups could be volunteers or selected at random. A random selection would be best, but this will require that the purpose of these sessions is clearly stated and that the confidentially of various positions voiced will be honored. This activity should be considered the first of a series of opportunities to talk about the importance of "teaching to the test." There will be additional activities dealing with this concept suggested in subsequent chapters of this book.

REFERENCES

Anastasi, A. (1976). *Psychological testing* (4th ed.). New York: Macmillan.

Archer, J. (2000a, June 21). NEA poised to debate pay for performance. *Education Week* 19 (41), 5.

Archer, J. (2000b, March 1). Georgia legislators pass accountability plan. *Education Week* 19 (25), 20.

Associated Press. (2000, July 30). Error found in grading tests. Jacksonville *Times-Union*, A13.

Boser, U. (2000, March 8). States face limited choices in assessment market. *Education Week* 19 (26), 1, 22.

Carnoy, M. (1999). Globalization and educational reform: What planners need to know. Paris, France: UNESCO, International Institute for Educational Planning.

Coleman, J., Campbell, E., Hobson, C., McPartland, J., Mood, A., Weinfeld, F., and York, R. (1966). *Equality of educational opportunity*. Washington, DC: Government Printing Office.

Dewey, J. (1928). Progressive education and the science of education. *Progressive Education* 5, 197–204.

De Nemours, DuPont (1812/1923). *National education in the United States of America*. B. G. DuPont (trans.). Newark: University of Delaware Press.

Ford, C., and Barta, P. (2000, January 18). Income gap broadens amid boom: Disparity of wages for rich and poor varies widely by state. *The Wall Street Journal*, A2.

Haladyna, T., Nolen, S., and Haas, N. (1991). Raising standardized achievement test scores and the origins of test score pollution. *Educational Researcher* 20 (5), 2–7.

Heilbrunn, J. (1996). Can leadership be studied? In P. S. Temes (ed.) *Teaching Leadership*, 1–12. New York: Peter Lang.

Hernstein, R., and Murray, C. (1994). *The bell curve*. New York: Free Press.

Hirsch, E. (1987). *Cultural literacy*. Boston: Houghton-Mifflin.

Hoff, D. (2000). As stakes rise, definition of cheating blurs. *Education Week* 19 (41), 1, 14.

Jaeger, R. (1992). Weak measurement serving presumptive policy. *Phi Delta Kappan* 74, 118–218.

Jensen, A. (1980). *Bias in mental testing*. New York: Free Press.

Johnston, D. (1999, September 5). Gap between rich and poor found substantially wider. New York *Times*, 14y.

Johnston, R., and Galley, M. (1999, April 14). Austin district charged with test tampering. *Education Week* 28 (31), 3.

Kincheloe, J. (1999). *How do we tell the workers? The socioeconomic foundations of work and vocational education*. Boulder, CO: Westview.

Kliebard, H. (1986). *The struggle for the American curriculum 1893–1958*. Boston: Routledge & Kegan Paul.

Linn, R. (2000, March). Assessments and accountability. *Educational Researcher* 29 (2), 4–16.

Madaus, G., and Kellaghan, T. (1992). Curriculum evaluation and assessment. In *Handbook of research on curriculum*, P. Jackson (ed.), 119–156. New York: Maxwell Macmillan.

Madison, G. (1990). *The hermeneutics of postmodernity*. Bloomington: Indiana University Press.

Mathews, J. (2000, June 19). A hot debate over summer schools. Washington *Post*, 29.

McGowan, J. (1991). *Postmodernism and its critics*. Ithaca, NY: Cornell University Press.

Mehler, B. (1999, Winter). Race and 'reason': Academic ideas a pillar of racist thought. *Intelligence Report* 93. Montgomery, AL: Southern Poverty Law Center, 27–32.

Mehrens, W., and Lehmann, I. (1969). *Standardized tests in education*. New York: Holt, Rinehart & Winston.

Meyers, E. and Rust, F. (2000, May 31). The test doesn't tell all. *Education Week* 19 (38), 34, 37.

Milken, M. (2000, September 5). Amid plenty, the wage gap widens. *The Wall Street Journal*, A34.

Mintz, J. (2000, May 1). A miracle or a mirage? Texas test scores have risen, but skeptics say the 'achievement gap' remains. Washington *Post National Weekly*, 6–7.

Miyasaka, J. (2000). A framework for evaluating the validity of test preparation practices. Unpublished paper, American Education Research Association. New Orleans, LA.

Popham, J. (2000). Teaching to the test: High crime, misdemeanor, or just good instruction? Unpublished paper, American Education Research Association. New Orleans, LA.

Popham, J. (1981). *Modern educational measurement*. Englewood Cliffs, NJ: Prentice Hall.

Raspberry, W. (1999, July 17). Teaching to the test—cheating or not? Washington *Post*, A8.

Robinson, G., and Brandon, D. (1994). *NAEP test scores: Should they be used to compare and rank state educational quality?* Arlington, VA: Educational Research Service.

Sacks, P. (1997, March/April). Standardized testing: Meritocracy's crooked yardstick. *Change*, 25–28.

Sanders, W., and Horn, P. (1994). The Tennessee value-added assessment system (TVASS): Mixed-model methodology in educational assessment. *Journal of Personnel Evaluation in Education* 8, 299–311.

Schick, R., DeMasi, M., and Green, M. (1992). Factors predicting writing performance. In A.C. Purves (ed.), *The IEA study of written composition II*, 153–168. Oxford, England: Pergamon.

Simonton, D. (1994). *Greatness.* New York: Guilford.

Stedman, L. (1994, October). Incomplete explanations: The case of U.S. performance in the international assessments of education. *Educational Researcher* 23 (7), 24–32.

Steffy, B. (1993). *The Kentucky education reform: Lessons for America.* Lancaster, PA: Technomic.

Tucker, M., and Codding, J. (1998). *Standards for our schools.* San Francisco, CA: Jossey-Bass.

Usher, R. and Edwards, R. (1996). Postmodernism and education. New York: Routledge & Kegan Paul.

Yardley, J. (2000, April 9). A test is born. New York *Times*, Section 4A (Education Life), 32–36.

Initiating Actions to Level the Competitive Playing Field

Creating a competitive level playing field for all children means assuring them that they will not be tested on knowledge or skills they have not been taught. Accountability tests are given for the purpose of formulating judgments about the efficacy of schools, teachers, administrators, and curriculum. There is no room for secrecy, and the instructional situation to be avoided is to surprise children. We call this the doctrine of no surprises (Frase and English, 2000, p. 19).

If an accountability test is to be a fair measure of what a child has learned, what his or her teacher has taught, and how the school is subsequently to be categorized and judged on the results obtained, then all children should have had a comparable opportunity to learn that which is going to be on the test. This idea means understanding that all children do not line up at the same jump-off point when the schooling process is initiated. In addition to students' varying maturational levels and natural inclinations towards school-based subjects, the powerful combination of these characteristics, comingled with cultural capital, results in situations where some children are distinctly advantaged in the schooling process from the very beginning (Kincheloe, 1999, pp. 245–246). Such children find school routines very much like their home routines. They are used to taking turns, sitting quietly, doing paper-and-pencil tasks, and manipulating computers, and their vocabulary and conceptual levels (based on "the curriculum of the home and the extended home") are already aligned with the schooling experience. Such alignment has been multiplied each year and leads to exponential results. Vocabulary and conceptual fields increase and expand rapidly.

Children from homes where intellectual–conceptual tasks have been neither dominant nor particularly valued, where middle-class politeness and values have not been emphasized, and where even the procurement of food has been marginalized are simply not going to be ready to engage in activities that appear to them to be unrelated to survival. Even in a booming economy, a recent report by the United States Department of Agriculture indicated that "31 million people grappled with hunger, or at least the fear of it" in America in 1999 (Reuters, 2000). Of these, twelve million were children and disproportionate shares were African American and Hispanic. Twenty-one percent of all African Americans "went hungry or lived on the edge of hunger in 1999," as did 20.8 percent of Hispanic people (p. 20).

Cultural differences between socioeconomic classes expose different patterns of resolving conflict. In many urban centers, argumentation between peers outside the home and on the street often leads to forms of physical aggression and fighting. Male-dominated, confrontational, urban street-culture survival skills are not conducive to largely middle-class classrooms, which emphasize quiet exchanges and concentrated mental tasks, which are the gist of standardized tests of accountability.

The black–white test score gap, which is one of the consequences of the lack of alignment with school tasks of inner-city African American children, is not "a fact of nature" (Jencks and Phillips, 1998, p. 2). Rather, it is a cultural construct, an invention of the differences among and within social classes accentuated by stark income differentials and the fallout of economic life in an increasingly income-polarized society.

The test score gap can be eliminated over time. Jencks and Phillips (1998) cite three reasons for their optimism in advancing this claim:

1. *Evidence of the Culture of the Home as Dominant*
   When African American children are raised in white homes, their test scores "rise dramatically" (Flynn, 1987; Neisser, 1998).
2. *Nonverbal I.Q. Scores Are Environmentally Sensitive*
   I.Q. tests are not measures that are indifferent to environmental alterations. Since the 1930s, I.Q. scores have increased all over the world. The implication is that "large environmental changes can have a large impact on test performance" (Jencks and Phillips, 1998, p. 3).
3. *Achievement Gaps Have Been Narrowing*
   Using data derived from the NAEP (National Assessment of Educational Progress), which has been utilized for nearly thirty years,

the black–white achievement gap has been narrowed (Jencks and Phillips, 1998, p. 3). We note, however, that recent trends in the NAEP again show a widening between scores of black and white students (see Hoff, 2000, p. 6).

The bottom line is that all children can be successful on state-mandated tests of accountability, though when these measures are mixed with privatization and voucher schemes, it is much more difficult. A study by Fiske and Ladd (2000) indicated that in New Zealand choice and competition were likely "to polarize enrollment patterns by race, ethnicity, socioeconomic status, and student performance" (p. 38). Such conditions already exist in many areas of the United States. However, we see no irreconcilable barriers that could not be overcome by educators who understand the differences between children caused by differential access to cultural capital. Children who receive low test scores should not be the product of poor instruction or cultural capital differences. The school is seen as the agency in which the playing field is leveled, without losing the enthusiasm of all children for learning and without penalizing anyone. The fear of the middle and upper classes is that alignment lowers some imaginary ceiling to the "level" of the poorer children, thus depriving their children of a stimulating learning environment. This is due to the fact that they cannot conceive of a learning environment in which anything but group-based teaching is not the single and only mode of instructional delivery. We know enough today about how to construct viable and stimulating educational environments so that all children are encouraged to apply themselves without penalizing any other children in the process.

FRONTLOADING OR BACKLOADING?

Once the decision to engage in curriculum alignment has been made, the question becomes where to start. Figure 3-1 illustrates a four-cell matrix representing four possible locations. Frontloading (English and Larson, 1996, p. 108; Steffy and English, 1997, p. 3; English, 2000, p. 65) refers to the linkage between curriculum development and assessment by initiating the process of alignment by creating the curriculum first and then working on the assessment process. This is the classical approach and it is the basis of nearly all local curriculum development. It only works, however, when a local school or school system has the power to write the curriculum and then determine which form of assessment is most appropriate to measure

Figure 3.1   The Four Faces of Curriculum Alignment

	design	*delivery*
frontloading	Write the curriculum first then write the test to assess it	Teach the curriculum first, then put it on paper and write the test to assess it
backloading	Obtain publicly released test items and create a curriculum from them	Obtain publicly released test items and create parallel classroom structures in which content/ context is embedded

the student learning expected to be derived from it. Such an approach is preempted when the state adopts its own test, with or without a state-created curriculum to which it may be aligned. When the state exercises this option, local curriculum development becomes superfluous because it may be possible to write a local curriculum with little to no alignment with the state test. In this scenario, the major contributing factors to good test scores are the SES-clustered variables, which are predictive of high test scores on unaligned tests (Wilkins, 2000). Eroding or erasing the predictive effects of SES-clustered variables means engaging in teaching what one is testing. If the state has no curriculum, or only a vague "curriculum framework" that takes the place of a detailed content domain, the resulting situation creates a large hole of ambiguity surrounding possible curriculum content and levels of contextual specificity in which frontloading is not a constructive alternative. There is too much guessing involved, and classroom teachers are not provided with sufficiently detailed contextual clues as to how to create high achievement-producing environments, which optimize student learning on such tests. Any time that SES-related variables are predictive and classroom-related variables are not, it is a sign that sufficient alignment was not present to offset them. In nearly all cases we know of, the problem was that the state had no curriculum or insufficient detail within their framework to enable classroom teachers to create learning environments that were sufficiently matched to the state's test to offset the predictive effects of SES variables affecting test performance.

By contrast, backloading (English and Larson, 1996, p. 108; Steffy and English, 1997, p. 3; English, 2000, pp. 70–71) is the process of starting to think about curriculum development from the test back to the curriculum. This makes sense when performance is defined, located, and situated within the assessment process as opposed to being defined, located, and situated in the curriculum. When a school is labeled as "low performing," the reference is not to a curriculum but to the tool or process of measuring performance, that is, the test. Backloading is a particularly attractive option when the curriculum to be assessed by the test is unknown or even a secret, as it is on most norm-referenced, standardized tests in use as state tools of accountability.

While backloading is often decried by the testing experts as a poor or even unethical practice because it results in inflated scores (see Miyasaka, 2000), when high-stakes tests are poorly aligned to curriculum practices, there are few other options open to local educators, which will actually lead to test score gains. Furthermore, our concept of deep alignment goes far beyond simply adjusting classroom practice to test items or test formats, which may result in only a one-year bump in test scores with a concomitant return to previous scores when the test is being changed annually.

We believe backloading with public, randomly released test items is the place to start, especially in working with teachers to develop broad understandings of how tests in use actually work and how, with the development of pedagogical parallelism, they can construct learning situations where not only tested knowledge is taught, but where teaching goes far beyond what any specific test item or format might assess in any specific assessment scenario.

Figure 3-1 also employs the terms design and delivery. By design, we mean the physical creation of a curriculum on paper before any classroom teacher would try to teach it. By delivery, we mean the teaching act or the implementation of the curriculum (English and Steffy, 1983). Here are the four options briefly described:

Frontload/design refers to the practice of creating alignment by writing the curriculum first on paper and then determining the most appropriate measurement tools in order to assess the expected learning results.

Frontload/delivery refers to the practice of creating curriculum by teaching first and then committing the curriculum to paper and adopting the measurement tools to be used to assess teaching effectiveness.

Backload/design refers to the practice of beginning the alignment process by working with publicly released test items from the assessment tool in use as the focus for writing curriculum. This is a more economical way to write curriculum, since it has a definite beginning and end which parallel the test objectives and content borders.

Backload/delivery refers to the practice of using publicly released test items as a way of constructing parallel classroom teaching situations, which include the content and context of the released test items as examples of how the test's objectives will be assessed. Classroom teaching should include but go far beyond such test items, especially when the test is being regularly changed.

CURRICULUM AS ORGANIZATIONAL MEMORY

Improving test scores on assessments of high-stakes accountability is a complex undertaking. First, schools were never organized for high-stakes testing or for learning. They were organized for order and for creating teachable situations for large masses of children. The search for cheap schooling has enjoyed a long history in American education, extending to the implementation of the Lancastrian School, which once held out the promise of efficiency (see Riddle, 1905, p. 82; Tyack, 1974, p. 41; Spring, 1986, pp. 53–54). Later forms were tried, such as the Platoon School. Many of the faces of accountability are primarily concerned with efficiency, that is, cost (see Callahan, 1962). Tests are seen as a method to drive efficiency and productivity into highly resistant forms of organization.

Anyone with a modicum of experience working in schools comes to realize how disjointed and complex schools are. While they are bureaucratic, they are also not internally tightly connected. One theorist has called them "loosely coupled" (Weick, 1976). By that term, he meant that there is not a chain of command that tightly links the bureaucratic offices to one another. Such couplings are present, but they are more akin to spheres of influence. Such spheres overlap, but there is not a command structure in which orders are communicated, as to be found in military command and control structures. This type of structure has a good deal of autonomy contained within it, even to the point where orders in the form of policies, procedures, rules, and regulations may be circumvented or ignored outright.

Although teachers are the chief persons who deliver the curriculum in schools, current work regulations, which are mostly informal in nature, provide them with a good deal of autonomy to proceed in ways that may be counterproductive to obtaining improved test scores on measures of high-stakes accountability. We view this as a structural problem rather than one that is internal to teachers. The history and tradition of teaching in most school settings is one that has not been linked to direct measures of their performance or the performance of their students. Furthermore, the trend to site-based management has been a major barrier to improved test scores, especially for secondary schools that must depend on their elementary counterparts to teach the curriculum that is subsequently tested at the secondary level.

High-stakes measures of accountability, especially when they are assessing complex learning, which must be acquired over many years of teaching and which is more cumulative in nature, require a kind of tight coupling which has not existed in most schools in the U.S. Such tight coupling lacks both a tradition and a history in American schools, especially when the tests in use are not direct measures of any specific curriculum or classroom. All of that changed when the tests in use changed. When tests become high-stakes measures of learning, one finds teacher resentment at their intrusive nature, especially when test administration dates require teachers to modify their preferred curriculum in use. Teacher complaints about the intrusive nature of tests, as well as the time such tests take away from classroom instruction, begin to crescendo. In England, there was a national teachers' boycott over the issue of greatly increased time involved with testing (see Firestone, Fitz, and Broadfoot, 1999, p. 768).

High-stakes tests require teachers to not only focus on what tests are measuring, but they require them to work together as they have never been required to do before. They require close, collective concentration on tested curriculum content, on assuring that the necessary horizontal and vertical connectivity are defined and utilized, and attention given to learners who have not made satisfactory progress. Figure 3-2 shows the differences between two kinds of curriculum connectivity: lateral, which is called *curriculum coordination*, and vertical, which is known as *curriculum articulation*. In the illustration, for a student to do well on the state twelfth-grade exit test, a vertically focused and connected curriculum must be in place which provides and promotes the necessary articulation to be present so that the complex learning that is tested is in fact taught all through the grades. If site-based management enables feeder schools to avoid teaching these basic skills, upon which more complex learning is required to do well on a twelfth-grade exit test, then site-based management is a hindrance to performing well on high-stakes tests of accountability. Such testing scenarios also require school administrators to lead teachers to engage in the kind of collective work that has not been standard practice in most schools before.

Figure 3.2   Horizontal/Vertical Alignment

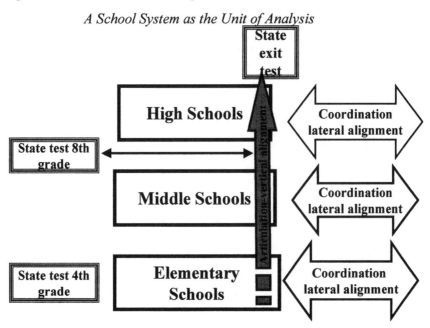

Against this historical backdrop it can be seen that curriculum design is also a matter of creating an organizational memory, a kind of written expectation in the form of a plan for not only what students should learn, but also of what they should be taught. To ensure maximum results on high-stakes tests of accountability, the content included on the test not only has to be taught, but the broad range of contexts in which learning could be assessed must also be taught. Both require multiyear teaching that is highly aligned to the tests in use. A curriculum is creating the road to get there and it provides a place to make notes of what worked and what didn't, as well as a place to connect test results. This connection enables curriculum workers and teachers to make subsequent changes in the work when it is to be done again. The curriculum is a kind of work record in this regard. Without it, there is simply no place to reconnect the information from tests that will be useful in altering what teachers do in classrooms. Think of the curriculum as the bridge that connects test feedback to classroom practice.

Two approaches to curriculum alignment should be considered. The first concerns creating consensus (not uniformity or standardization) at some horizontal point in a school, such as a grade level or a series of grade levels (for example, the primary unit concept, K–3). In this circumstance, teachers create shared curricular plans, which may be disciplinary (subject centered) or multidisciplinary (involving more than one skill or subject center). This is curriculum coordination work. Such work may consist of developing curriculum units or activity or interest centers. Such centers should be embedded with those concepts, skills, and dispositions that are also found on the state accountability tests.

The other approach, which may also be a parallel activity, is to create work groups that consist of vertical teams. In a research study by Miles and Darling-Hammond (1998), they found that a creative definition of staff roles and work schedules, as well as more common planning times for staff, were two of six principles of resource reallocation strategies that earmarked high-performing schools (p. 12). Vertical teaming involves both of these principles. Such groups are created in recognition that a sample of learning on any test involves much prior learning. For example, a test given in the first three months of the fourth grade is testing more of the K–3 curriculum than the fourth grade. The fourth grade is merely the test administration point. Once test items are disaggregated, it may be seen that children performed poorly not because of any deficit or problem in the fourth grade, but the lack of sufficient learning in grades K–3. In this respect, though tests may be administered at specific administration points, the tests themselves are assessing all prior grades. In this scenario, every teacher's work is being assessed, not merely the teachers working at grade levels where the tests were administered.

WHERE TO START THE ALIGNMENT PROCESS?

The decision to initiate curriculum alignment work should be a practical one. If there were no pressure to raise test scores, then the preferred strategy would be to engage in frontloading, that is, writing a curriculum first and devising the assessment strategy next.

We advocate frontloading using national and international standards as qualitative benchmarks for the simple reason that such comparative indicators enable educators to engage in evaluative activities that speak to such matters as curriculum rigor and quality, which are open and public and do not depend on a secretive content domain that is nobody's specific curriculum. In short, our approach is not aimed at improving norm-referenced, standardized test scores. We view norm-referenced, standardized tests as inappropriate measures of curriculum rigor and quality because such tests avoid these issues altogether by reporting student scores compared to one another instead of to public and specific curricular benchmarks. Furthermore, we view education as a process of deciding upon appropriate curriculum content and activities as anything but a random measure. Tests that conceptualize learning as random cannot be tools upon which to establish measures of accountability. In short, we reject the bell curve as the appropriate statistical frequency distribution for purposes of accountability. Most norm-referenced, standardized tests tell us more about the demographic characteristics of the students taking them than they do about the curriculum that the students did or did not learn (Jensen, 1980, p. 724).

STEPS IN DEVELOPING A FRONTLOADED CURRICULUM

We now sketch out the steps in developing curriculum from a frontload. The purpose of the steps is to produce a frontloaded, written curriculum document aligned to national/international benchmarks that focus on student mastery and can be delivered in the amount of instructional time available.

The development of a frontloaded curriculum alignment guide that meets national and international standards is a process that requires substantial preparatory and follow-up work. We have divided this work into three phases: preparation, actual writing, and implementation/feedback and evaluation. Within each of these phases, a number of steps must be completed. We recommend that a curriculum design team be established to oversee each of these phases. If the curriculum alignment document being developed is to be used to define the district-mandated, board-approved, core curriculum for a given content area, such as K–8, the design team should include teacher representatives from elementary, middle, and high schools. These teacher representatives should be at the expert/master level, receive the endorsement of peers and administrators, and be willing to make a multiyear commitment to the project. Their role would be advisory in nature and they might or might not serve on the committee that actually develops the guide. In addition, representatives from a variety of other stakeholder groups in the system might serve on the design team. These members could represent specific areas such as special education, media, or alternative education. The addition of board members, parents, and student representatives is at the discretion of district administration. The number and role of central office and building-level administrator participants are dependent on the size of the district and the availability of staff. Some districts may want to include business leaders and representatives from higher education on the design team.

If the curriculum alignment project has a more narrow focus on a specific course, the design team may be much smaller and may complete all phases of the process.

Phase One—Preparatory Work

The design team should review data produced from the following activities, summarize the information, and prepare a briefing report for the curriculum writing team.

Step 1: Assembling Resource Materials   Assemble resource documents to be used by the committee actually developing the alignment document. These should include the latest edition of national standards published by learned associations, model state frameworks, and international standards from countries noted for high levels of student achievement in the curriculum area under development. The annual fall publication of "Quality Counts," printed by *Education Week,* is a rich source of information regarding the quality of state standards. Most state standards are available from state department of education web sites and can be easily downloaded. Additional standards documents are available through the regional offices of national labs and organizations. Publicly released test items from a variety of national and international sources should also be assembled. These can include test items from the National Assessment of Educational Progress, International Baccalaureate, Advanced Placement Exams, state graduation assessments, state criterion-referenced tests, and assessments given in other industrialized nations such as England, Scotland, France, Germany, and Japan to name a few.

These materials serve to provide the design team with an understanding of what knowledge, dispositions, and performances other states and nations view as important. From this review, the design team should prepare a summary report outlining the nature of process and content expectations for an internationally based curriculum.

Step 2: Review Student Achievement Data   Review all data regarding student achievement for the past five years. If the area under development is part of the state or district accountability system, these data should be disaggregated to include achievement by level, ethnicity, gender, and SES. The format, content, and use of assessment data within the system should be summarized and provided to the design team. If the content area under development has no measure for assessing levels of student achievement, the design team should prepare a recommendation outlining what data may be collected and how these data might be used to evaluate the program over time. The development of a program evaluation component will become part of the task of the document writing team.

Step 3: Conduct Literature Review   Conduct a review of the literature to determine current "best practice" regarding pedagogy in this area. Prepare an annotated bibliography of the literature review for use by the writing team. Describe current programs that have been identified as exemplary models.

Step 4: Identify Future Trends   Identify future trends occurring within the content area and project the direction of these trends. This is especially important in areas such as the impact of technology and information access, in order to develop the skills students may need to master in the future.

Step 5: Revisit Current Board Policy Regarding Curriculum Management Does board policy require a focus on critical thinking and problem solving? Do policies speak to the required balance among three types of curricula: content knowledge, process knowledge, and curricula serving a social need? Does board policy require curriculum documents to identify mastery-level student achievement? We strongly recommend that written curriculum documents state what students should know and be able to do at mastery level at benchmark points such as at the end of elementary school, middle school, and high school. Further, these documents should specify how teachers, parents, and students would know that mastery has been achieved using multiple measures. These could include the use of a portfolio complete with scoring rubrics. Benchmark mastery through this process provides an environment of "no surprises" for children. As educators, we owe students the opportunity to have access to information about what will be used to document mastery, complete with the scoring rubrics used to make the determination. Students also need to be assured that they will have an opportunity to participate in a learning environment designed to ensure that they will achieve these standards. If present board policies are not clear on this subject, the design team should make recommendations to the administration regarding changes in board policy and administrative regulations to ensure that once the curriculum guide is developed, board policy mandates that it will be utilized by teachers to plan instruction and by administrators to monitor the implementation of the curriculum.

Step 6: Prepare Status Report of Current Instructional Materials   Current instructional materials should be reviewed and a summary prepared that includes data regarding the age, content, and suitability of these materials for further use. Additionally, any current curriculum guides should be reviewed and rated using a rating system that takes into consideration objectives, evaluation, scope and sequence, materials, and suggested teaching strategies.

Step 7: Develop Work and Guide Specifications   Develop specifications for the work of the curriculum writing team. Include time parameters, guide format, team representation, support for the work of the team, a mechanism for communication regarding the work of the writing team with the rest of the faculty, and resources available to the team. Many of these components will depend on the type of guide being developed. There is an expectation that the guide will include some basic components. These include objectives stated with enough specificity to enable a teacher to know what is expected of students and yet not so discrete as to deal with isolated skills. It is best to think of these objectives as end-of-year "big ideas" of what students leaving a grade can do at the mastery level that they could not do upon entering the grade at the beginning of the year. The written guide should include estimated time ranges for the amount of instructional time required for most students to achieve mastery. This requirement is made not to mandate the amount of instructional time teachers are to use in teaching the skill, but to prevent the developers of the guide from creating a document that contains far too many objectives to be taught than the amount of instructional time available to teach them. We refer to this phenomenon as creating a bomb bigger than the plane to fly it. The bomb is the written curriculum and the plane is the amount of instructional time available. All objectives that are presently assessed as part of the district/state accountability system should be coded so those teachers understand that these objectives must be mastered before the assessment is given. Major instructional materials should be identified by reference and page number so that teachers know exactly where material addressing the objective is located. The guide should include a scope and sequence chart so that teachers know what objectives students were required to master in prior grades and also what objectives teachers at higher grades expect students to have mastered. Finally, as a basic minimum, the guide should include suggested instructional strategies that have been determined to be effective in teaching these objectives in the past. The design team may want to consider an additional column in the guide that will enable teachers to make comments and offer suggestions during the guide implementation. Most districts now have the capability of placing curriculum guides on a networked information system so those teachers can input these data at their computer terminals. We consider the items discussed here to be basic and necessary, but the design team may also want to consider additional information. Figure 3-3 shows a format for these basic components.

Figure 3.3   Basic Format for Curriculum Guide

Objectives	Time	Primary Instructional Materials	Sample Test Items	Cues
What is to be taught including content and cognitive level?	Time ranges for student mastery	Referenced by resource and page number	Coded to district and state assessments. What is it students will have to know and do, including format (context)?	Suggestions for teaching strategies. Adaptation required for alignment.

Phase Two

Phase Two should be completed by the curriculum writing team. The members of this team should include representatives from the design team, but the expertise needed for this phase includes comprehensive knowledge of the content area and the ability to write objectives that capture the "big ideas," yet provide the specificity teachers need to design instruction. The team should include representation from all grades covered in the guide. The team should have a designated chair or cochairs who are responsible for providing an overview for the work, organizing the work sessions, and dealing with problems along the way. It should be clear to all members of the writing team that the activities have been carefully planned and it is possible to accomplish the work in the amount of time available. Normally, this process takes six months to an academic year.

Step 1: Provide the Writing Team with an Overview of the Task   The writing team should receive an overview of the work that has been accomplished by the design team. They should also be made aware of the work that will take place in Phase Three of this project. Finally, the chair of the committee should provide an overview of the curriculum management process, including the concepts of design/delivery; written, taught, and tested curriculum; and articulation/coordination.

Step 2: Developing a Framework for the Curriculum Guide   There is always more to teach than there is time to teach it. One of the major problems with current curriculum guides is that they contain more objectives than can be addressed in the amount of instructional time available. It is much easier to address this problem at the beginning of the guide development process than to finish a guide and realize that it contains too many objectives to be achieved at mastery level. One way to address this problem is to engage in a concept attainment exercise to identify the major areas or strands to be addressed in the guide and then determine the amount of instructional time to be devoted to each strand at each grade level.

Begin the activity by asking each member of the team to identify the five most important things students should know or be able to do at mastery level for the grade level taught. These should be written on regular-sized sheets of white paper, one statement per sheet with the grade level indicated, and placed on a blank wall with masking tape. If the committee included twelve members, there would be sixty sheets on the wall when the task was completed. Then committee members are encouraged to see if any of the statements cluster together. If they do, the clusters should be assembled and labeled. If the committee was developing a K–8 guide for social studies, for example, typical cluster labels may include geography, history, communities, culture, and research. This activity is useful in not only identifying the strands for the guide, but it enables every committee member's voice to be heard and allows the committee to get to know one another.

After the strands are identified, there should be a discussion about whether additional strands need to be included. At this point, it may be necessary for the chair to review the strands included in internationally benchmarked curriculum, the state framework, or the strands used in the state assessment system. At the end of this discussion, there should be a consensus agreement that the K–8 curriculum guide in social studies will be designed using the agreed-upon strands.

Step 3: Setting Time Parameters   Next, the committee should determine the amount of instructional time available to teach the material in the guide at each grade level. Starting with kindergarten, the committee is asked to specify the approximate amount of instructional time devoted to social studies. Typically, assuming a full-day kindergarten, teachers specify about twenty minutes a day for social studies. By first grade, the time is increased to thirty minutes a day. This increases to forty-five minutes a day by sixth grade, and continues at forty-five minutes a day through eighth grade.

The team is then asked to specify the percentage of the time available at a grade level to each of the strands. Through this activity, the team begins to see how very limited they are in the number of objectives to be achieved at a given grade level and how important it is to be sure that the objectives at one grade level fit with the objectives at the next grade level.

New learning is cumulative and difficult. They need to be reminded that the grade where an assessment measures student achievement is not necessarily where students learned the objective. It is also at this point that the committee needs to be reminded that the objectives included in this curriculum guide are objectives to be achieved at mastery level. The guide is not one that includes enabling objectives, enrichment objectives, or extensions. This curriculum guide includes core, mastery-level objectives that all students are expected to achieve. This core curriculum guide becomes the accountability document for judging the effectiveness of the system. Designing a curriculum guide with more objectives that students can achieve at the mastery level ensures failure from the beginning. A well-constructed guide, with objectives that are doable empowers teachers to focus and connect instruction thus expanding the number of students demonstrating mastery. Figure 3-4 shows the results of a typical social studies guide framework, including the consideration of teaching time available and percentage of focus for each of the strands.

Admittedly, this is a gross estimation. However, it does serve the purpose of driving home the realization that instructional time is limited. Time may be our most valuable resource in schools. For instance, if there are 30 minutes of instructional time available per day for social studies at the first-grade level, and geography objectives consume 30 percent of this time, it means that whatever the objectives listed in the guide dealing with geography must be able to be achieved at mastery level in approximately 27 hours of allotted time. The research on time utilization in schools tells us that, of the allotted time, only about 50 percent of it is actually engaged

Figure 3.4   Social Studies Framework and Time Allocations, K-8 Curriculum Guide

Instructional Time Available	Strands With Percent of Instructional Time Used				
	Geography	History	Community	Culture	Research
K–20 min.	25%		50%	25%	
1–30 min.	30%	15%	30%	15%	10%
2–30 min.	30%	20%	20%	15%	15%
3–40 min.	25%	20%	15%	20%	20%
4–40 min.	20%	25%	10%	20%	25%
5–40 min.	20%	25%	10%	20%	25%
6–45 min.	15%	30%		30%	25%
7–45 min.	15%	40%		25%	20%
8–45 min.	15%	40%		25%	20%

learning time, so we are down to 13½ hours to achieve our objectives. Add to this the fact that we do not want our core curriculum guide to consume 100 percent of the instructional time available and we have even less time to achieve the objectives.

Some may protest this approach by saying that the state framework includes many more objectives than can be accomplished and teachers currently are trying to cover all of the objectives in the state framework and not working for mastery of a small number of objectives. We believe the correct approach is working towards mastery of an articulated, coordinated curriculum. The above activity enables the committee to see just how important it is to work towards mastery and be mindful of what is expected of students at each grade level.

Step 4: Balancing Content and Process Focus   The next limiting factor that needs to be discussed by the committee is the amount of focus on content and process to be included in each of the strands. It is common to see a heavy focus on content at the middle and high school levels and less of a focus on process. Typical statements of what students should know at the high school level in social studies include: "Explain the steps leading to the development of the Constitution," or "Identify the factors leading to World War II." Retention of factual knowledge is known to be short-lived. Most board policy statements about what students should be able to do upon graduation include problem solving, critical analysis, and the ability to take a position and support it. To achieve these latter objectives, content becomes the vehicle not the outcome. The committee will have to decide on general guidelines for balancing both process and content needs.

Step 5: Determining Benchmark Achievement   At this point, the committee has created a framework for the guide, estimated instructional time allocations for the strands in the framework, determined the approximate percentage of emphasis on each of the strands, specified the balance between content and process focus, and endorsed the concept of mastery-level attainment for objectives included in the guide.

The next task involves identifying what students would show as evidence for attainment of the objectives at given benchmark points in the program. We recommend that these points include exiting elementary school, middle school, and high school. Some committees have chosen to include benchmarks at the end of third grade as well as the end of elementary school. The decision is up to the committee. The important point here is to specify as precisely as possible what evidence students would present to demonstrate mastery. We further recommend that these demonstrations be a collection of artifacts included in a portfolio. Portfolios would be formally presented to teachers, peers, significant stakeholders, and others the students chose to include. The portfolio could include videotape of oral presentations, test scores on criterion-referenced tests, research papers, journals, written summaries, narratives, reflective commentary, and projects. The committee should brainstorm what artifacts should be included in the portfolio that would demonstrate mastery of essential skills in the content area under development. Once developed, this listing becomes a way to focus the development of specific objectives for the areas identified in the strands. If, for instance, an artifact to be included in a portfolio for an exiting eighth grader was a fifteen- to twenty-page research paper and Power-Point oral presentation describing a culture that identified the major events influencing the development of the culture in the areas of art, science, education, economics, and politics, utilizing both primary and secondary sources, then knowing this would provide direction for the development of the objectives to be attained in prior grades. This type of artifact would address not only one strand but integrate the social studies strands along with strands that may be included in English, fine arts, and other content areas.

By identifying the artifacts, committee members begin to see how the content areas are interdependent. It is all too common for one content area teacher to register concern that another content area teacher did not prepare students to do the things the first teacher expected students to be able to perform. Unless these objectives are written down in the core curriculum and there is an expectation for mastery, some students will have the skills and others will not. In these situations, teachers are forced into using valuable instructional time to reteach or teach for the first time the skill needed to complete a desired assignment.

Step 6: Using a Q-Sort to Narrow the Focus of the Written Curriculum The Q-Sort is a useful activity to delimit the content of the curriculum covered. This technique is best used when developing a curriculum for a specific course such as Chemistry I and all the teachers who teach Chemistry I are involved in the development process. Begin this activity by calling a meeting of all of the teachers involved and explaining the task. Provide teachers with as many 3x5 cards as they want and tell them to write a single topic, a concept for skill they think is important to teach in that course (or grade level). Schedule the second meeting within a few days and have the teachers bring their cards. For the purpose of providing an example, let us assume there were five teachers teaching Chemistry I. At the second meeting, the chair of the committee asks for someone to begin. The first teacher begins to read off the notations for his/her cards. The first may deal with the concept of bonding. The chair asks if anyone else had written down the concept of bonding. Assume all of the teachers had, so this topic goes in a stack called *fives*, meaning all five members of the committee felt that this was an important concept. The next concept may have had only two teachers identify it. This topic would go in the twos pile. This process would continue until all of the topics/concepts/skills were presented. That would be the end of the second meeting. Between the second and third meetings, someone would type in alphabetical order the topics in each of the piles and have copies of these for review at the third meeting.

At the third meeting, the committee would review the topics in the fives stack and possibly the topics in the fours stack to determine whether there was agreement. It would be at this meeting that the philosophical discussion would take place about those things that are most important to be learned in Chemistry I. Committee members would have an opportunity to change their designation during this meeting.

Following this meeting, the committee chair would develop a validation matrix for the topics chosen. A validation matrix is simply a chart that lists the topics down the left side of the page and then lists validation sources across the top. If the topic identified were part of the national standards for that area, then a check would be placed on the matrix. If it were part of the state assessment system, a check would appear. The sources for validation are up to the committee and the weights given to each source are also up to the committee. Through the validation matrix, the committee is attempting to be sure that what the committee feels should be in the curriculum is validated by other learned organizations.

The final activity for this step is to estimate the amount of instructional time necessary to reach student mastery of the concept/topic/skill. The time estimates are done two ways. First, determine the minimum and maximum amounts of time necessary to reach mastery. Add up the two columns and determine if the average amount of instructional time available is sufficient. If it is not, some concepts may be removed, some may be added to other curriculum content area objectives, or the amount of instructional time may be expanded through homework. Through this activity, we are once again dealing with the idea that the bomb (core curriculum) must fit into the plane (amount of instructional time available).

Step 7: Writing Outcomes That Include Content, Context, Cognitive Level, and Level of Performance   Now it is time to write the outcomes for each strand of the curriculum in a way that will provide teachers with the specificity they need to plan instruction. The committee must remain mindful of the amount of allotted instructional time available for the delivery of the guide. (See Step 2, Phase One.)

There are four major components of a well-written outcome: content, context, cognitive level, and standard of performance. All four components are necessary. Most state frameworks include objectives that state the content and the cognitive level. The content states what the student should know and be able to do, and the cognitive level is linked to *The Taxonomy of Educational Objectives: Handbook 1: Cognitive Domain* (Bloom, Engelhart, Furst, Hill, and Krathwohl, 1956). Knowledge level content is at the lowest level of the taxonomy. For instance, an objective that reads, "Students will list [cognitive level] the capitals of the fifty states [content]" is at the lowest level of the taxonomy and asks students to recall facts. "Students will name [cognitive level] the steps in the scientific process [content]" is another example of an objective requiring recall. Objectives requiring students to use higher levels of Bloom's Taxonomy include the following: "Students will use stated criteria to assess the strengths and weaknesses of political decisions." "Students will be able to state a position and defend it." Statements such as these would be placed in the first column of the suggested guide format. The remaining two components of a well-written outcome become the basis for the design of sample test items and go in the fourth column (sample test items). These two components include context and level of performance. The context tells the teacher the conditions under which the behavior will be performed. For instance, if the objective was "to take a position and defend it," students may be asked to write a short paragraph given an open-ended response item such as this: "Coal has been discovered under the town park. As a member of town council, would you vote to mine the coal and destroy the park or would you vote to save the park? State your position and defend it."

When the context is described, teachers have a better understanding of exactly what students will have to do to verify mastery of the objective. The final component of a well-written outcome is the level of performance required for the designation of mastery. This can also be included in the sample test item column. In order for consistency in determining mastery across teachers, scoring rubrics and cut-off scores have to be determined. All four of these components (content, context, cognitive level, and standard of performance) should be clear and concise. Teachers are then in a position to understand exactly what students are expected to do in order to demonstrate mastery of the objective.

After all of the objectives have been written and sample test items created, the next step is to identify the time ranges necessary for student mastery (see explanation under Step 5) and determine whether it is possible to deliver the curriculum as designed in the amount of instructional time available. Make the necessary accommodations based on this review.

Step 8: Faculty Validation   It is now time to share the emerging guide with all faculty members who will be affected by the guide. Prepare a memo from the curriculum writing committee stating that a new curriculum guide is being developed in the area of ___(subject)___. The memo could read as follows.

> This guide identifies objectives and provides sample test items to determine student mastery. It also includes estimates of the amount of instructional time necessary for student mastery of the objective. Review the objectives, time estimates, and sample test items. Indicate whether you agree or disagree with this listing. If you agree, simply check here. If you disagree, indicate to the committee how the objective(s), time range, or sample test item should be changed. Sign this form and return these materials to the building principal by ___(date)___.

The writing team will review this feedback as part of the process for completing the guide.

Step 9: Completing the Guide   Instructional resources with page numbers and cues should be completed in the appropriate columns. The cues column may include suggested teaching strategies or adaptations teachers need to make to align instructional materials with the content and context of the outcome. This column can also be used to collect information from teachers as they implement the guide. Provision for this is best done on computer.

Phase Three

Step 1: Piloting the Guide   All new curriculum guides should be introduced through an initial pilot program. If the guide is for K–8 students, then teachers from all nine grades should be involved in the pilot. It is preferred that some teachers from each building join in the pilot, assuming separate buildings, so that when the guide is implemented throughout the system, teachers who have been involved with the pilot program can be used to aid the rest of the staff.

It is best to ask for volunteers for the pilot. Teachers who served on the design team and writing team are expected to participate in the pilot. The length of the pilot is at the discretion of the administration, based on a recommendation by the design team. Questions to be answered include the following:

- Are the outcomes clear (objective + sample test item[s])?
- Are the time ranges realistic?

- Are the materials identified in the guide appropriate and accurate?
- Are there additional materials available that are not listed in the guide? If so, identify them.
- Are additional instructional materials needed? If so, what and where are they available?
- Are sample test items helpful in enabling the classroom teacher to determine what mastery means?
- Are additional test items needed?
- Are scoring rubrics and cut-off scores available? If not, can they be developed?
- Does the guide include suggested instructional strategies? If so, are they appropriate?
- Does the guide describe how present instructional materials need to be modified to assure alignment?
- Additional comments, questions, and suggestions.

After the pilot has been completed, the curriculum writing committee will reconvene and review feedback from the teachers. Modification will be made in the guide and it will be finalized for distribution to all of the faculty.

Step 2: Providing for Total Faculty Input   The curriculum writing team will design a process for providing faculty input while the guide is being formally implemented. This could take the form of building focus groups. Each focus group will be chaired by someone who served on either the design team or the curriculum writing team. Focus group chairs will meet together to design a series of structured interview questions to guide the discussion of the focus groups. Focus groups will meet every two months during the first year of implementation. A district secretary will attend each focus group meeting and prepare a summary of the discussion. Possible questions for the focus group session can include many of the same questions used in the pilot.

Another way to involve faculty is by placing the guide on the district web site and enabling faculty to enter comments about the implementation of the guide over the course of the implementation year.

Step 3: Program Evaluation Design   Most systems do not have adequate program evaluation designs. If no program evaluation design exists for the content area addressed by the guide, one needs to be developed. The following list suggests criteria for program evaluation (permission to reprint granted by CMAC of Huxley, Iowa).

1. Program evaluation procedures are outlined in board policy and/or administrative regulations.
2. Procedures for program evaluation include needs assessment, formative evaluation, and periodic summative evaluation.
3. Persons conducting the evaluation are both trusted and competent, ensuring that findings achieve maximum credibility and acceptance.
4. Multiple measures of data collection are used, including quantitative and qualitative measures.
5. Reports clearly describe the program, its context, purposes, procedures, findings, and recommendations.
6. Reports are utilized to make timely decisions regarding program effectiveness and continuation.
7. Program evaluation designs are practical, cost effective, and adequately address political issues.
8. Report identifies both strengths and weaknesses of the program.
9. Data used to evaluation the program are accurate and reliable.
10. Procedures used in the evaluation are clearly described.
11. All programs are evaluated every three years.

If a program evaluation design is in place, periodic reports to the board should be made regarding the effectiveness of the program. During the first two years of implementation, the program evaluation should be formative in nature. This means answering the questions: "Is the program being implemented as designed?" and "If not, why and what changes need to be made?" At the end of the third year, a summative evaluation should be made that is linked to increases in student achievement. This means that a mechanism for determining student achievement at the mastery level must be developed. This can include both quantitative and qualitative data from students, teachers, and parents.

Step 4: Professional Development Plan Professional development plans for the content area addressed by the guide must be based on teacher-identified needs related to the implementation of the guide. For instance, if teachers are having difficulty designing instructional strategies to ensure student mastery, professional development sessions should focus on providing teachers with these skills. Determination of this need could be the result of feedback from the focus groups, based on a needs assessment distributed to teachers, or the result of a recommendation by building administrators based on their observations of curriculum implementation.

Step 5: Documenting Exemplary Practices   We believe that the best source for exemplary practice is teachers within the system. Measures should be developed to identify and capture these exemplary models for implementation of the curriculum. Most districts have the capability of producing high-quality videotapes of classroom teachers in action. Based on administrative recommendation or teacher nomination, episodes of exemplary instruction related to the implementation of the curriculum should be recorded. These videotapes could be used to assist new teachers, provide models for existing teachers, serve as exemplars of best practice for the community, used at state conferences, and shown on the district's web site.

As the bank of exemplars grows, the expectation is that all teachers implementing the curriculum will be expected to teach at these high levels.

By the end of the fourth year, summative data should be available to document student achievement and the effectiveness of the program. If the textbook adoption process is on a five-year cycle, it is time for a new design team to be put in place and the cycle begins again.

KEY CONCEPTS OF THIS CHAPTER

Backloading   The practice of creating alignment between the written and taught curriculum with the tested curriculum by beginning with the tested curriculum; used in situations where the curriculum is not specific except in global frameworks or other amorphous standards

Cultural constructs   Concepts or ideas that have a specific root or axis in a specific culture, and which may be lightly regarded or unknown in other cultures

Curriculum articulation   The focus and connectivity of the curriculum vertically within a school or school system. This can be discipline specific or interdisciplinary in nature, and is most important for test scores at the secondary school level.

Curriculum coordination   The focus and connectivity of the curriculum laterally at any designated point as in the case of a grade level or series of grades in the primary unit (for example, K–3)

Design   Any activity in creating curriculum that results in it becoming a written document

Delivery   Refers to any activity involved with implementing the written curriculum

Doctrine of no surprises   The idea that children should not be taken by surprise by any test question; that is, because of the fact that teaching includes more than what is on the test, the student knows how to tackle the types of problems likely to be encountered on any high-states accountability test

Frontloading   An approach to curriculum alignment, which begins with developing a curriculum and then selecting the appropriate measuring tool to assess it

Loosely coupled   The concept that organizational layers in schools and school systems are not tightly connected to one another, leaving room for some autonomy on the part of each person's role in relationship to other persons. Although school systems may look like they are linear command structures, such depictions belie their very uneven and fragmented role connectivity.

Tightly coupled   Refers to roles in an organization that are tightly connected by a chain of command; such organizations are hierarchical and commands usually run from top to bottom

Organizational memory   The capacity of persons in an organization to recall why certain actions or precedents occurred and the meaning they have or had for the organization at the time

APPLICATIONS

1. Beyond Curriculum Guide Development

Purpose: The purpose of these activities is to initiate a process for informing the system about trends and patterns that will affect future curriculum development activities, and establish a professional development process that enables all teachers within the system to grow and develop.

Step 1: Form Futures Committee   Form a futures committee. The role of this committee is to identify and track trends that may influence all facets of future education. Membership on this committee should be by recommendation of a current district administrator or highly positioned public official or business leader. Membership should be kept to approximately twelve to fifteen participants, with rotating memberships of four years. All initial members of the committee will serve at least three-year terms, with some members serving four- and five-year terms to permit a smooth transition of membership. Committee members should receive a yearly stipend for their work, comparable to stipends paid to athletic coaches.

Committee members will be charged with keeping district administration and board members apprised of future long-range trends and patterns that will have an impact on public education ten years in the future, with interim projections five years into the future. Committee members may represent more than one content area or specialization. For instance, one member may be charged with tracking developments in science and mathematics. Another may have responsibility for technology. A third could be assigned the areas of special education, school–community partnerships, and parent relations. A fourth may specialize in building construction, funding formulas, and school design. A fifth member may specialize in global economics, population trends, and future careers. The possibilities are limitless.

Initially, the committee will need to become conversant with the futuring literature. Their primary responsibility is to identify and track possible future developments, and to interpret how these developments may affect the local school system. As these trends and patterns begin to have an impact on the learned organizations of our field, members will focus on their areas of specialization. While this committee is advisory in nature and reports to the superintendent or his designee, the committee is expected to make formal reports to the board each year outlining both five and ten-year trends and make recommendations for both board and administrative consideration.

Step 2: Develop Hiring Plan to Reflect Future Trends   When a new teacher is hired, the district is making a commitment for more than twenty years. Since it is highly likely that a new teacher employed by the district in the year 2000 will still be working in the system in the year 2010, consideration should be given not only to the skills the teacher brings to the system today, but the propensity of the new teacher to possess the skills the district will need in 2010. Characteristics such as technological literacy, global outlook, and foreign language proficiency are just a few skills that are important now, but may become mandatory in the years to come.

Personnel officers in the system should take the yearly reports produced by the futures committee and prepare information briefs detailing how the trends and patterns identified may have an impact on the future personnel needs of the system. For instance, if there is a trend toward expanding employment opportunities for migrant workers within the community, and the trend is for this need to be filled with Hispanic workers, then it will be exceedingly important to hire Hispanics not only because of their fluency with the language but to serve as role models for students. If this trend is deemed to be large, the district may want to recruit support staff such as paraprofessionals and aides from the Hispanic community, and to work with local or regional colleges to develop a certification program for needed staff. If the community is not near a local college, it may be necessary to develop a relationship with a university via distance learning to offer the degree. All things are possible given enough lead time to plan for the future needs.

Step 3: Project Future Remodeling/Construction Needs to Accommodate Future Trends   Future trends can also have a significant impact on the design and expansion of facilities. Using the example above, if the district plans an expansion of the use of distance learning for staff training or to accommodate the ability to offer a wide variety of courses with a small class size, there may be a need for a series of rooms where this instruction can take place.

Flexible class configurations will be essential to accommodate both large group instruction and small work groups. Access to technology in each classroom will, no doubt, become commonplace. Construction that will accommodate schools within a school will become the norm. Teacher work areas will be expanded to include teams of teachers needing access to a variety of planning materials. These units will be available at a variety of places around the school, not just isolated in one area.

Step 4: Establish Communication Network with Outside Networks   This function could be assumed by the futures committee or assigned to a specialized group. Basically, this group would link with three large national networks: the regional educational labs, the major educational publications, and the national associations. All three initiatives would be responsible for the publication of a quarterly newsletter that would highlight the issues, innovations, and initiatives currently being pursued or written about. These newsletters would be available to all employees in the district via the district's web site. Since all three of these areas are actively involved or report current and projected grant opportunities, this initiative is especially important for making faculty aware of innovative funding opportunities to support accommodation of future trends.

Step 4: Establish a Conference Watch Task Force   Most districts have no organized plan for conference attendance. We recommend that this area offers a unique opportunity to support conference attendance that complements the work of the futures committee. Conference attendance should be approved to support gaining information that will enable the district to maintain a cutting-edge perspective. Serious consideration should be given to the prospect of sending someone to the American Educational Research Association annual conference. This meeting is considered the premiere educational research meeting in this country. Presenters include the most noted researchers and theoreticians in our field. The reject rate for proposals at this conference is somewhere between 70 and 80 percent. The organization mandates that research presented at the conference be unpublished. What one generally finds is that the initial presentation of research takes place at AERA. Then articles are written about the research. Given time, a collection of articles may become a book or a special issue of a scholarly journal. As the research begins to have an affect on practice, additional articles appear in trade journals such as *Educational Leadership, School Administrator,* or *Instructor Magazine.* It usually takes several years before the field adopts an idea. In keeping with the idea of maintaining cutting-edge knowledge, the type of conferences attended by school personnel should be a balance between conferences where new knowledge is being presented and conferences where theory is being translated into practice.

Once conference attendance has been approved, there should be a plan for communicating what was learned at the conference with the rest of the district learning committee. Common practice now is for someone to attend a conference and that individual benefits and may influence a few others. The idea here is that a select few will attend specifically chosen conferences and subsequently influence the thinking and planning of the entire district based on what was learned.

The synergy that can be produced by this type of activity is enormous. Classroom teachers have ready access to the latest thinking of national experts in their field. Teachers recognize that the district values continued growth and learning on the part of everyone within the organization. Everyone knows that the knowledge acquired through this activity will affect future decisions made by the board and administration to improve the quality of education within the system.

Step 5: Create a Culture That Supports a Positive Professional Development Community   Many school districts promote a district culture that supports the maintenance of the status quo. Once hired, teachers are expected to grow and develop, but the culture of the system does not make it clear that this is an expectation for every person employed, not a matter of choice for a few that thrive on growth. Developing this type of growth culture is based on the recognition that all teachers in the system are not at the same point in terms of their life cycle. The life cycle model is a modification of a career stage model developed in the late 1980s (Steffy, 1989). It is based on the premise that teachers need different opportunities for professional development based on their career stage. The present model identifies six phases. The first phase, called the *novice phase,* begins while the teacher is still in preservice training. The next phase is labeled the *apprentice phase*, beginning when the newly certified teacher becomes employed as a classroom teacher. This is followed by the *professional phase* and we claim that the majority of classroom teachers are at the professional phase. The next phase is called *expert* and refers to a teacher who meets two criteria: (1) this teacher meets the requirements for national certification in his/her area and could successfully gain this certification if he/she chose to, and (2) this teacher consistently creates a learning environment that enables her/his students to score high levels of achievement no matter what accountability system is in use. It is our estimate that currently about 20 percent of the classroom teachers in this country fall into this phase. Our goal is to support activities that will enable districts to assure that 80 percent of the teachers in the system are at this level. The next phase is called the *distinguished phase*. Teachers in this category are recognized nationally and at the state level for their contributions to our field. Teachers recognized as teachers of the year typically fall into this category. Our final teacher phase we call *emeritus*. These teachers are those who have retired from the profession but keep active in the field as political advocates for education, classroom volunteers, and mentors for apprentice teachers.

Teachers move from one phase to the next through a cycle of reflection, renewal, and growth. Some teachers are able to create this supportive cycle for themselves, but these tend to be the exceptions. Almost 40 percent of the newly certified teachers hired leave the field within the first five years of employment, abetted by forces within the system causing the teacher to go into withdrawal. Some studies suggest these may be our most intelligent teachers, based on their college entrance exams. The key to keeping these teachers in the field may be related to the ability of the system to provide the necessary professional development activities to enable these teachers and others to perpetuate the reflection, renewal, and growth cycle.

Using this model, an administrator can set high expectations for teacher growth and development, and provide teachers at all phases of development with growth activities that keep the cycle going.

REFERENCES

Bloom, B., Engelhart, M., Furst, E., Hill, W. and Krathwohl, D. (1956). *The taxonomy of educational objectives. Handbook 1: Cognitive domain.* New York: David McKay.

Callahan, R. (1962). *The cult of efficiency.* Chicago: University of Chicago Press.

English, F. (2000). *Deciding what to teach and test: Developing, aligning, and auditing the curriculum.* Thousand Oaks, CA: Corwin Press.

English, F., and Larson, R. (1996). *Curriculum management for educational and social service organizations* (2nd ed.). Springfield, IL: Charles C. Thomas.

English, F., and Steffy, B. (1983, February). Differentiating between design and delivery problems in achieving quality control in school curriculum management. *Educational Technology* 33 (2), 29–32.

Firestone, W., Fitz, J., and Broadfoot, P. (1999, Winter). Power, learning, and legitimation: Assessment implementation across levels in the United States and the United Kingdom. *American Education Research Journal* 36 (4), 739–793.

Fiske, E., and Ladd, H. (2000, May 17). A distant laboratory: Learning cautionary lessons from New Zealand's schools. *Education Week* 29 (36), 56, 38.

Flynn, J. (1987). Massive IQ gains in 14 nations: What IQ tests really measure. *Psychological Bulletin* 101 (2), 171–191.

Frase, L., and English, F. (2000, March–April). When doing more means doing nothing well. *Thrust for Educational Leadership* 29 (4), 19.

Hoff, D. (2000, September 6). Gap widens between black and white students on NAEP. *Education Week* 20 (1), 6.

Jencks, C., and Phillips, M. (1998). The black–white test score gap: An introduction. In C. Jencks and M. Phillips (eds.), 1–55. *The black–white test score gap.* Washington, DC: Brookings.

Jensen, A. (1980). *Bias in mental testing.* New York: Free Press.

Kincheloe, J. (1999). *How do we tell the workers? The socioeconomic foundations of work and vocational education.* Boulder, CO: Westview.

Miles, K., and Darling-Hammond, L. (1998, Spring). Rethinking the allocation of teaching resources: Some lessons from high-performing schools. *Educational Evaluation and Policy Analysis* 20 (1), 9–30.

Miyasaka, J. (2000). A framework for evaluating the validity of test preparation practices. Unpublished paper, American Education Research Association. New Orleans, LA.

Neisser, U. (ed.). (1998). *The rising curve: Long-term gains in IQ and related measures.* Washington, DC: American Psychological Association.

Reuters (2000, September 10). Millions still going hungry in the U.S., report finds. New York *Times*, 20.

Riddle, W. (1905). *One hundred and fifty years of school history in Lancaster, Pennsylvania.* Lancaster, PA: Published by the author.

Spring, J. (1986). *The American school 1632–1985.* New York: Longman.

Steffy, B. (1989). *Career stages of classroom teachers.* Lancaster, PA: Technomic.

Steffy, B., and English, F. (1997). *Curriculum and assessment for world-class schools.* P. Short (ed.). Lancaster, PA: Technomic.

Tyack, D. (1974). *The one best system: A history of American urban education.* Cambridge, MA: Harvard University Press.

Weick, K. (1976). Educational organizations as loosely coupled systems. *Administrative Science Quarterly* 21, 1–19.

Wilkins, J. (2000, April). Characteristics of demographic opportunity structures and their relationship to school-level achievement: The case of Virginia's standards of learning. Unpublished paper, American Education Research Association, New Orleans, LA.

• 4 •

Engaging in Deep Curriculum Alignment

$\mathcal{T}$he concept of alignment is disarmingly straightforward, as shown in figure 4-1. The three forms of curriculum in school settings are: written, taught, and tested. These forms may exist at any unit of analysis within schools: classrooms, grade levels (for elementary or middle schools), departments (for high schools), schools, or school districts. Within each one, the educator can establish coordination and articulation. When these facets are analyzed, the written expression of them is curriculum design. The expression of their implementation is curriculum delivery. The connectivity between all three has both content and context. When all of these elements are matched, we have engaged in deep curriculum alignment. This phrase helps differentiate at least two conditions: (1) a condition in which there is a partial presence of the conditions but not all, and (2) a condition in which they are all present and are operational. The litmus test is always this: has the condition resulted in consistent score gains on the test(s)? (see Pogrow, 1999) The presence of consistent test score gains is also the meta–criterion for deep curriculum alignment.

Although the three elements of deep curriculum alignment may be present, each represents dissimilar proportions or weights. Such a condition is shown in figure 4-2. The largest curriculum is the taught; the next largest is the written; the smallest is the tested.

The reason for these proportions is clear to anyone familiar with schooling. Teachers try to capitalize upon the teachable moment. Such moments are opportunities that are child-centered, that is, they arise from the children and not from the curriculum. Such moments may be prompted by something the children have seen or heard on television: a disaster of some

Figure 4.1   The Concept of Curriculum Alignment Nested in Three Levels of Organization

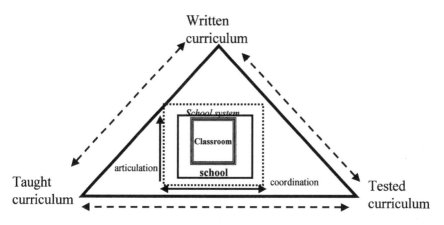

Figure 4.2   Relative Proportionate Emphasis of the Three Types of Curricula

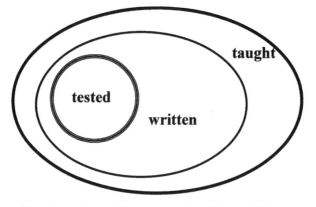

The doctrine of "no surprises" for children

sort, such as a hurricane or an earthquake; a scientific discovery about dinosaur remains; the location of a Spanish galleon loaded with silver and gold off the shore of Florida; or a scientific breakthrough represented by a cure for a disease or some new discovery in space. Such events may stir children's imaginations and emotions. Experienced teachers understand that such moments present golden opportunities to stress the importance of clarifying concepts, searching for the facts, learning new vocabulary, and making important connections to prior classroom learning.

Such deviations from the expectations of the written curriculum, if they may be called that, are simply good teaching practices. The capability of harnessing the interests of children in something they find absorbing to important prior or ongoing learning can work wonders in classrooms by lifting the spirits of both teachers and students. The curriculum too often contains inert ideas (Whitehead, 1959, p. 1) sent into the minds of children "without being utilized, or tested, or thrown into fresh combinations" (p. 2). This situation may be particularly true with abstract concepts that have become reified, that is, to be learned because they are considered "real" instead of symbols. Some of these facts may be dry as dust. The most vital learning, learning which is remembered and applied in novel situations to be found in life and perhaps on tests, is learning that is fresh and immediate and that connects to the everyday experiences of the children. As Alfred North Whitehead has observed, such learning must come to the learner "just drawn out of the sea and with the freshness of its immediate importance" (1959, p. 147).

The next proportionate element is the written curriculum. The written curriculum is the plan of work. Although it may contain a variety of pieces of information, our last chapter illustrated what elements are crucial to success in improving pupil test scores. We have also commented on the peculiar American climate for curriculum writing in which, in the absence of a national curriculum, the standardized test makers have filled the void. They have created a surrogate for content domain and have bypassed key decisions, such as what would constitute a passing score, by filling in with percentiles based on "typical" student responses within a specified norming sample. We think the "cure" for the lack of a truly national curriculum in the form of norm-referenced, standardized tests is worse than the disease it was designed to combat. This historical response has created an educational Hydra, a multimillion-dollar testing industry (Boser, 2000) that functions as a huge social sorting machine for the nation's children, shrouded in a cult of secrecy, wrapped in the mantle of scientism, resting on a foundation of racism, which is antithetical to democratic values and good classroom teaching practices (McNeil, 2000).

The tested curriculum is the smallest part of the three elements, though in practice it may carry the greatest weight in accountability schemes. Tests sample the curriculum (or content domain). Economies of testing mean that there is not an unlimited amount of time to engage in classroom testing, nor is it profitable to create a test that is unduly long or tedious. For this reason, nearly all tests do not try to assess everything that could or should have been learned, but only those things that are considered to be most important or even typical. Because of these limitations, the test makers and those using their products usually desire to generalize from the sample to the whole content domain (or curriculum, as the case may be). Thus, a math score on a standardized test including math concepts and skills actually represents a small part of the total math content domain, but the score is considered representative of the total math content for a designated grade level.

We have already commented at length about the function of secrecy in this model. The confidence of a generalization about test results depends upon the extent to which one can be sure that the sample of the content domain within the test has not been divulged (in the jargon, kept "secure"). When this is not the case, the veracity of the generalizations about the score of the tested content representing the larger domain is undermined. If the content domain on a test has been divulged, instead of being able to represent that score as indicative of the entire content domain, we are able only to express the score as representing the sampled content and may have no idea how well a student would do within the larger domain.

Behind this concept is the idea that there are important underlying skills, concepts, or themes in the respective curriculum subjects. A curriculum subject area is comprised of a kind of conceptual scaffolding in which a learner must function. Various theories of cognition attempt to explain how this works but it is beyond the scope of this book to differentiate among them. Suffice it to say that for the typical educational practitioner, the tested curriculum is proportionately the smallest of the three represented in deep curriculum alignment. However, it may exercise an importance that belies its stature in the overall scheme of things.

THE EMERGING RESEARCH
ON CURRICULUM ALIGNMENT

One finds scattered about in the research literature ideas that could be called *curriculum alignment*. Zellmer (1997) has indicated that he believes the term *curriculum alignment* was created by the Southwest Research Laboratory in Los Angeles when they were working with the Los Angeles city schools to improve pupil performance in the early 1980s (p. 37). The terms *instructional alignment* and *curriculum overlap* were earlier terms that contained the notion of curriculum alignment. Zellmer's (1997) literature review traced work dealing with curriculum overlap to Husen (1967) and Chang and Raths (1971). Floraline Stevens (1984) has indicated that curriculum alignment began as a process utilized in court-ordered school desegregation to improve the quality of instruction at selected elementary schools. Crowell and Tissot (1986) discussed the need for curriculum alignment within the process of curriculum development.

The first statewide effort reported in the research literature was by Cohen and Hyman (1991) in Missouri. Disappointed with norm-referenced testing, the Missouri State Department of Education moved to develop a statewide curriculum followed by a statewide test (the MMAT—Missouri Mastery Achievement Test). Dramatic gains were recorded involving 60,000 students. The state supplied over one hundred school systems with sample, alternative MMAT items as exemplars. Within two years, the so-called normal distribution of test scores had disappeared, indicating strong construct validity.

The Zellmer Study

Michael B. Zellmer (1997) undertook a study of curriculum alignment in the Milwaukee area at Marquette University. The purpose of his study was to determine what the results would be on test scores of selected third-grade students when their teachers were provided information about the test in use (p. 15). Zellmer was also testing what he termed an alignment technique that filled "the need for an inexpensive treatment that can be produced in a short period of time" (p. 16). Noting that many curriculum-alignment efforts require extensive commitment over long periods of time, Zellmer was interested in determining if there could be a shorter, cheaper route (p. 16).

Zellmer randomly selected twelve school districts. Then he randomly selected two teachers from each district. By coin flip, he assigned one teacher to an experimental group and one to a control group. He had twelve classrooms of third-grade students for each of the two groups. The total number of students in his study was 533.

Zellmer's inexpensive treatment consisted of packets of information about the test (the Wisconsin Reading Comprehension Test) as follows:

- Data regarding how many objectives, skills, and goals were actually assessed on the WRCT;
- A statement of how many of the objectives, skills, and goals are assumed on the test but not directly tested;
- The number of objectives, skills, and goals from the local curriculum document that are not directly tested;

- Those objectives, skills, and goals that were tested most frequently on the WRCT were shown for key test areas;
- The frequencies and percentages of all the test items that were categorized by type were shown in charts and explanations;
- Additional data about the "district-specific" curriculum-alignment information contained analytical results of the "types of words, punctuation, and sentences that were found on the 1995 and 1996 WRCTs" (p. 69). For example, the listings included all words over seven letters, unusual or difficult words, examples of punctuation methods, and tallies of different sentence types;
- Zellmer also provided succinct descriptions about the thinking, skill, and internal reading problems that were required to answer each question. "The information provided in two of three sections in each district's curriculum alignment information document was referenced to the local reading curriculum and was written in local terminology" (p. 70).

When the packets of information were mailed to the experimental teachers, the teachers provided certain raw data to Zellmer about the students' past reading scores and gender. But, significantly, teachers were not asked to do anything with the data, that is, they were not asked to alter any instructional practices. They were explicitly informed to use their own judgment about such matters (p. 70). Three times during the year, Zellmer sent questionnaires to each teacher in the experimental group querying them about their use of the curriculum-alignment data in their classrooms.

The results of Zellmer's 1997 study showed that there was "no significant difference between the mean test score of the control group and the mean test score of the experimental group" (p. 77). In fact, the control group outscored the experimental group. The results are not shocking. Teachers receive a lot of data about a lot of things. Being busy persons, they attend to what they must. Clearly, there were no expectations for them to do anything different in their classrooms with Zellmer's alignment data, and his study showed that they didn't make any radical alterations in their teaching with the data. For example, in a follow-up questionnaire, Zellmer asked his teachers in the experimental group some questions about their use of the data. A majority indicated that they did consult the alignment data (92 percent); emphasized certain reading skills in other content areas (78 percent); emphasized some areas of the regular curriculum less (81 percent); emphasized some skills, such as modeling some procedures like re-

reading some areas, for clarification (75 percent); and modeled how to make inferences for students (56 percent).

Areas in which the teachers in the experimental group responded negatively were that they did not consult their local curriculum document more frequently (66 percent); did not use the alignment data in selecting supplementary materials (75 percent); and did not alter the time of year that they introduced or taught anything (71 percent) (pp. 84–85).

It is significant in Zellmer's study that (1) no specific instructions or expectations were given to teachers in the experimental group about how to use the alignment data, when to use it, or how it would be valuable to improve pupil achievement, and (2) school principals were not active participants in the study. Zellmer's "inexpensive" approach to alignment involved no staff development for teachers in the experimental group. They had no models to follow and what exactly they did with the data was not described beyond Zellmer's questionnaire information. In commenting on future research, Zellmer said that it should address "the level of use of the 'treatment' more systematically" (p. 95).

We think that Zellmer's study demonstrated that there is no cheap way to utilize curriculum alignment without a well-developed approach to staff development, modeling how to apply the data in the classroom (pedagogical parallelism), and the systematic use of supplementary materials. The reason is that the main source of teachers' daily work is the textbook, and textbook/standardized test alignment has been notoriously low. For that piece of the alignment puzzle, we turn to Price-Baugh's (1997) dissertation research.

The Price-Baugh Study

Ricki Price-Baugh's study (1997) took place in the Houston Independent School District, Houston, Texas. Houston is the fifth largest urban school system in the nation. Its enrollment is over 190,000 students, of which 57.7 percent are classified as economically disadvantaged based on free lunch applications. The ethnicity of the student population was 49.2 percent Hispanic, 35.7 percent African American, 12.2 percent Anglo, and 2.9 percent Asian, with the remainder Pacific Islander and/or American Indian (p. 44).

The purpose of the Price-Baugh study was to ascertain "if a positive non–zero correlation existed between the alignment of the textbook with student achievement scores on the Texas Assessment of Academic Skills (TAAS)" (p. 108). The study involved seventh-grade math scores for

English-proficient students not classified in special education. The textbook used in her study was Scott, Foresman and Company's *Exploring Mathematics: Grade* 7 (Bolster, 1991). The student population for Price-Baugh's research was 10,233 seventh graders enrolled in thirty-five middle schools. The overall passing rate on the TAAS was 40 percent (p. 45).

Price-Baugh examined both content and context alignment. Textbook content subdivided TAAS targets that defined content possible for testing components. Price-Baugh simply counted the number of skill-level and application-level word problems in each target component. She then used a Spearman *r* to "correlate the amount of practice and explanation in the textbook for 11 tested target components with the percentage of students correctly answering TAAS problems on those target components" (p. 109).

Price-Baugh's results showed that all of the textbook variables included in her analysis significantly correlated to student achievement on the target components assessed with skill-level items, except location in the textbook of the practice items for each target component. Of particular importance was the finding that 56 percent of the variance alone was explained by the "number of available skill-level practice items in the textbook for each target component" (p. 111). The number of pages devoted to practice problems was found to be statistically significant at the .02 level and explained over 68 percent of the skill-level variance (p. 111). Most important in Price-Baugh's study was that application-level problems included in the text studied had a 0.83 Spearman *r* to TAAS skill-level achievement and explained over 68 percent of the variance in skill-level achievement (p. 113).

Price-Baugh indicated that accountability and pay plans for teachers were dubious since they did not select their own textbooks and many did not know what the alignment was to the test of the book they were using. The teacher cannot be held responsible for supplementing textbooks with low alignment if they are not supplied with the data. Looking back on Zellmer's (1997) study, the textbooks teachers were actually using were not part of his study. Supplementing texts with low alignment becomes important. Zellmer's teachers in the experimental group did not use the data he supplied for this purpose. The importance of alignment data as school system personnel consider textbook adoption practices may be even more significant than providing teachers with alignment data because teaching practice in the U.S. remains textbook dependent. Price-Baugh cites the work of Freeman and Porter (1988), who found in examining elementary teachers in three different districts that the "textbook had the most influence in teacher determination of the topics and their sequence of presentation" (p. 34). Text exercises were used 92.2 percent of the time when the teacher used the book.

The Moss-Mitchell Study

Felicia Moss-Mitchell (1998) conducted her study of curriculum alignment with over 4,000 third-grade students in DeKalb County, Georgia. Georgia is considered a high-poverty state for children in age ranges five to seventeen. About 22 percent of the school-aged children in Georgia are poor. Moss-Mitchell (1998) estimated that 55 percent of the 50,000 elementary pupil population in DeKalb County were poor by the free and reduced lunch count (p. 7). DeKalb County is part of the twenty-three-county metropolitan area of Atlanta.

The purpose of the Moss-Mitchell study (1998) was "to examine the implications for educational administrators of effectiveness of the DeKalb County school system's curriculum alignment after one year of implementation" (p. 8). The measure selected to determine improvement was the Iowa Test of Basic Skills (ITBS) at one grade level (third) and in one subject (mathematics). The Georgia legislature had mandated the ITBS. It does not "match" the Georgia curriculum nor does it align with any local curriculum.

Moss-Mitchell's research questions were these:

- What is the difference between DeKalb third-grade students on the ITBS in mathematics before and after curriculum alignment?
- What is the difference in the performance of third graders on the ITBS in mathematics when they are matched on socioeconomic status?
- What is the difference in the mathematics performance of third graders on the ITBS when analyzed by gender?
- What is the difference in the mathematics performance of third graders on the ITBS when analyzed by school size? (pp. 18–19)

In setting up her study, Moss-Mitchell included all third-grade students in DeKalb County for whom there were 1997 ITBS scores that could be compared to their 1996 ITBS second-grade scores. No repeaters of the third grade were used in the sample and non-English speakers were also excluded (p. 62).

Socioeconomic status in the Moss-Mitchell study was defined as the percentage of free and reduced lunches received by school (p. 63); school size was defined by three categories (normal 200–800; large 800–1000; very large 1000+). Race was selected by Moss-Mitchell because of the data she cited, which showed that in 1992, 64 percent of school-age children (from six to seventeen) living below the U.S. poverty line were African Americans (p. 69), and that race was a factor in previous curriculum-alignment studies, which showed that it benefited African American students, but had a negative impact on white students (Lynch, 1990).

The curriculum-alignment process utilized in DeKalb County consisted of two approaches. Evans-Newton, Inc., of Scottsdale, Arizona developed one (Moss-Mitchell, 1998, p. 84). Four schools adopted this model, which was centered on "intense staff development, monitoring, and managing" (p. 84).

The other approach used a three-step process beginning with the identification of district goals and the correlation of the textbook in use with the ITBS. It was found that 23 percent of the content in the textbook did not match the ITBS (p. 85). The third step of the process involved creating or selecting additional curricular reference materials that "filled in the gaps" (holes in the textbook/test match) (p. 86).

Moss-Mitchell employed the use of organized staff development through instructional coordinators. Such persons were responsible for six elementary schools and presented the concept of curriculum alignment as a way to improve student test scores on the ITBS. Copies of the aligned curriculum were grouped into a specific notebook. Copies were placed in every public library in the school system (p. 87). School principals were also involved.

The results of the one year intensive work on curriculum alignment showed "that there was a six-point NCE gain, from 49 to 55, in the 4,665 scores of all matched third-grade students on the Iowa Test of Basic Skills" (p. 96). More importantly, "there was no statistically significant difference in the effects of curriculum alignment after one year of treatment when analyzed by socioeconomic level, race, gender, or school size" (p. 96).

Moss-Mitchell summarized her research by saying that "there were desirable gains despite the traditional predictors of poor student achievement: low socioeconomic status, being black, being male, and learning in a school with over 800 children" (p. 100). Moss-Mitchell viewed her results as "providing a format for creating equity in curriculum development" (p. 103) and curriculum alignment "is a flagship of hope as it emerges as 'the instructional equalizer'" (p. 105).

We see in the Moss-Mitchell study how the DeKalb approach was different from that used by Zellmer (1997). The ingredients in the DeKalb model not present in Zellmer's approach were:

- A highly focused model (Evans-Newton, Inc.), which brought together textbooks and tests and which provided the basis for local curriculum development to "fill in the gaps;"
- The assignment of specific instructional supervisory personnel who were charged with implementing the model;
- A focused staff development program, which used the local curriculum materials;
- The development of local notebooks, which included important alignment information and which were made available to the public;
- The involvement of school principals.

In short, the difference between the two approaches is that Moss-Mitchell's 1998 approach was much more systemic and comprehensive in nature. Obviously, it was more costly as well. We see no shortcuts here. Alignment can work, but cheap alignment, which consists only of providing information to teachers without the support of supervisors and administrators is not likely to be effective.

THE PRACTICE OF PEDAGOGICAL PARALLELISM

Pedagogical parallelism refers to the notion that classroom teachers create an alternative but parallel environment in which their students not only learn what is on the test, but learn more. The teachers go deeper than the tested curriculum content. To create such a parallel environment, teachers must clearly comprehend the nature of tests and the ways (formats) children must think in order to be successful within them.

We have not found that such thinking represents any kind of normal practice for teachers. In fact, most teachers have been warned repeatedly not to go anywhere near the test, except to give it in as antiseptic a situation as possible, something akin to holding up a frog in a jar of formaldehyde. As a result, the general teacher outlook regarding the use of information derived from state tests (particularly norm-referenced tests) to improve classroom practice has been completely sterilized (see Bright,

1992). Occasional media stories about teachers or principals being fired for cheating or using tests inappropriately have created a toxic professional environment for considering salutary practices in regard to using test data constructively. Our experience is that since teachers generally do not understand the reasons for secrecy surrounding tests, they have created a professional cultural taboo against using them at all, except administratively (as in recording the scores on various kinds of school records). The expanding use of tests in this kind of environment is viewed as an increase in the police power of the state in order to fire teachers who have students with low test scores. Such an outlook also contributes to blaming the victim, meaning that low test scores are the result of "dumb students." The victim (usually poor and of color) is conceptualized as genetically inferior (see McNeil, 2000). Another corollary practice is to track or stream these students to a less challenging curriculum. The result is a vicious circle in which lower expectations produce lower test results (see Gamoran, Porter, Smithson, and White, 1997).

The idea of pedagogical parallelism is based on assumptions of transfer, which harken back to Edward L. Thorndike (1913). Briefly recapitulated, transfer is enhanced when situations are identical. Test performance, which is supposed to be representative of classroom performance, is one kind of transfer situation. Test performance is therefore enhanced when students have an opportunity to practice that which the test is assessing. Two aspects of transfer are important: (1) the content of the situations; and, (2) the contexts (formats) of the situations. The practical implication is that students should not only have an opportunity to learn the knowledge on the test in the classroom, sometimes called *declarative knowledge* (Phye, 1997, p. 49), but learn how it is to be assessed on the test. The latter means that students should be familiar with the different types of formats that the test may employ to assess their knowledge, sometimes called *procedural knowledge* (see Phye, 1997, pp. 48–50). Such pedagogical parallelism must go on year-round as standard classroom practice, and not just be employed a month to a week prior to testing (see Miyasaka, 2000).

A STEP-BY-STEP GUIDE TO PEDAGOGICAL PARALLELISM AS THE KEY TO DEEP CURRICULUM ALIGNMENT

Instituting pedagogical parallelism in classrooms means accepting the idea that the test should contain no surprises for children. We think this is especially appropriate when a wide range of judgments will be made based on the test results, not the least of which are judgments about the children themselves, as well as their teachers and their schools. These steps can be done individually or in a group.

Step 1: Backloading from Public, Randomly Released Test Items

We advocate beginning the process of deep alignment by obtaining copies of the public, randomly released test items from the state department of education. This is the approach to creating alignment via backloading. The reasons this method is especially apropos are: (1) most state frameworks are silent on the matter of assessment approach, that is, what kinds of test items will be typical for students to encounter. This context piece is a crucial part of doing well on high-stakes tests of accountability; and (2) being able to practice the behaviors required on a test ahead of time means that the classroom teacher must be able to construct learning situations that include those behaviors and then move beyond them.

A very practical matter for classroom teachers is to come to grips with the question, "How deep is deep?" Only a sample test item can answer this question adequately. We never let the matter rest there, however. To use a swimming analogy, it should be clearly understood from the beginning of creating deep curriculum alignment that the publicly released test item is the equivalent of the shallow end of the pool. Our expectation is that the public, randomly released test item provides an operational definition of "test deep," but given the probability that the test will be changing, to exclusively teach to such released items only works if the test is stable. Teaching to public, randomly released test items may produce a brief bump in scores, but fail to produce the consistent gains that are the hallmark of deep alignment over time.

Step 2: Deconstructing Public, Randomly Released Test Items

Begin this step by disaggregating the public, randomly released test item. The process is shown in figure 4-3.

The test item is systematically deconstructed by engaging in the analysis shown in each window of the matrix. List the concepts and vocabulary required to do the item (these may overlap to some extent), then list the knowledge and skills required. Item distractors are of two types: (1) poorly constructed questions that are ambiguous, and (2) good questions that have more information present than required to complete the problem. The last step is to write an alternative test item that is comparable to the one that

Figure 4.3   The Process of Deconstructing a Public Randomly Released Test Item

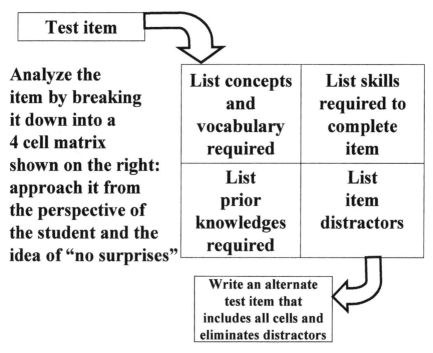

has been released. Being able to write a good, comparable test item is an excellent check on whether one understands what is being asked of students. In writing the comparable item, eliminate the distracters due to poorly constructed test questions. Often at this point it is not uncommon to realize what aspects have been taught or not taught in regard to the knowledge being assessed.

A sample fifth-grade test item is presented in figure 4-4. Identify the vocabulary, knowledge, and skills a student would have to know in order to successfully answer the questions. When you have completed your individual list, share it with a partner. This always generates a great deal of discussion and the lists are usually rather long. Next, engage your partner in a discussion about what they listed. One of the first things listed is always direction. Students would have to know about direction. Probe a little to get them to be specific about direction. The skill here could be stated as follows: "When given two directions on the compass, students will be able to determine the other two directions." Probe with your partner (or a

Figure 4.4   Map Reading Test Item

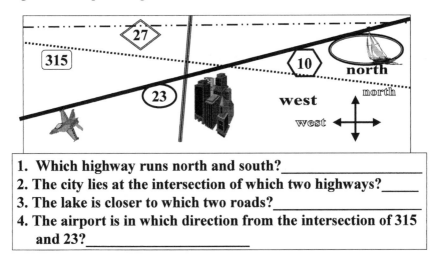

1. **Which highway runs north and south?**_____
2. **The city lies at the intersection of which two highways?**_____
3. **The lake is closer to which two roads?**_____
4. **The airport is in which direction from the intersection of 315 and 23?**_____

group of colleagues) to determine where direction is currently introduced and mastered in the present social studies curriculum. Most will say that direction is introduced in the first grade, but they are not sure where it is mastered. Some say first grade, some say second. When asked where it appears in the curriculum, most are not sure. Another typical skill mentioned is: "Students will be able to interpret symbols on a map when the symbols are presented in different ways." It is also mentioned that there is no key on this map and students would first have to know how to use a key before they could infer what the key might be. For instance, four different symbols are used to denote roads or highways. Probe again with the group to get them to identify the pre-skills necessary to be mastered in order to successfully answer the questions. Because this is an item from a fifth-grade test, what skills would students need to master at grades one, two, three, and four in order to be ready to handle this item? The symbols used in this item are not ones commonly used in map-reading materials. For instance, the symbol for the airport is unusual as is the one for the city. Students would have to be taught that different symbols could be used to denote the same thing. Again, ask the question about where these skills appear in the present curriculum and how teachers determine that mastery has been achieved for each grade level.

Next, read the objective/standard cited in the state framework that this item is assessing. For one state, the objective/standard was stated as follows: "Students will be able to read maps." Then go to the testing company's listing of objectives upon which the test was developed. The objective stated here is as follows: "Students will be about to interpret maps." Neither statement provides teachers with the specificity they need to design instruction. Test item disaggregation provides teachers with the knowledge to understand not only the content assessed but the context as well.

Finally, ask yourself, your partner, or your group if they have the expertise to teach the skills necessary to be successful with the type of test item. Of course, they answer "yes." When asked if they need new instructional strategies before they could teach these skills, they usually say "no." When asked if they need a new learning theory from a college professor, they definitely say "no." When asked if they need new instructional materials, most say they feel comfortable modifying the instructional materials that are already available. In other words, teachers feel confident that they can teach the skills students need to successfully answer a question like this one when they understand what skills are being assessed and the context of the assessment and are reassured that teachers in prior grades have taught the pre-skills to mastery.

Additional test items should be disaggregated until you have a clear understanding of how to complete this activity. If you or your participants represent a variety of content areas and grade levels, you should bring sample test items to disaggregate. These test items should include ones students would have to answer at higher grade levels so that teachers begin to see how what is accomplished at one grade level affects the next.

Step 3: Developing Alternative Test Items

One of the problems with state assessment systems is that the format or context of the state assessment system is different from the format or context of the assessment system used by classroom teachers. If a teacher typically prepares tests that require short essay responses, students become skilled in how to handle this form of assessment. If the state assessment system uses a multiple-choice format, students may not be able to make the transfer from one assessment format to another, and thus they are surprised. As stated earlier, the objective is not to surprise our students.

Consequently, we recommend that teachers develop alternative test items utilizing their present instructional materials and utilize these items throughout the school year so that when a student is presented with the format on the high-stakes accountability system, the student is not surprised.

In a forty-five-minute work session, teachers can be taught to disaggregate public, randomly released test items. Using their instructional materials, it is easy for them to construct alternative test items that require the application of the same skills using different content. These sessions can be designed so that teachers working in small groups design test items, review and critique those developed by the group, and select the best ones for inclusion in a test item bank available to all teachers in the system.

Although these types of materials are currently available from publishers, they tend to be unrelated to the specific instructional material teachers are presently using. Without the direct connection of the content being discussed in the classroom, they tend to take on a "drill and kill" quality. However, if the practice items are routinely integrated into ongoing classroom instruction and directly linked to the content, they become another strategy for instruction, as opposed to simply test preparation (see Miyasaka, 2000). Used in this way, along with a wide variety of testing strategies, they enable students to learn how to handle multiple types of assessments, thus getting closer to the concept of deep alignment.

If you are working with teachers on developing alternative test items, this is a good way to check their understanding of what students are actually required to do, as opposed to guessing about it. A good alternative item is a good check of the teacher's understanding of the learning and curriculum that is going to be assessed.

Step 4: Identifying Test Item Distracters

Almost all test items include distracters. For multiple-choice test items, these can often include such things as including extraneous information, formatting irregularities that are unfamiliar to the student, phraseology that can be confusing, and answer choices such as "all of the above" and "none of the above." Sometimes distracters are simply poorly written test questions that leave even prepared students guessing as to what is actually desired as a response.

We recommend reviewing a wide variety of publicly released test items to identify common distracters. Once identified, teachers need to teach students how to deal with common test item distracters. Starting as early as third grade, students can be taught to analyze test items for distracters and taught strategies to deal with them. Teachers need to include these common distracters in the test items they create in order to get students used to dealing with them.

In the last step, teachers were taught how to develop alternative test items to enable students to transfer their learning from the classroom situation to the testing situation. These test items may or may not have included distracters. Now teachers are taught to develop alternative test items that include distracters. Again this can be done in small groups and another series developed and included in the district's test bank.

Step 5: Test–Textbook Alignment

After you have a solid grounding in the content and context of the state assessment system, you are ready to determine the level of alignment between the tests and the textbooks, including primary supplemental materials. Given the current trend among textbook publishers to cover many topics superficially, we often find that the state assessment system is assessing student achievement at a much higher level than the way material is presented in grade-level texts.

For this step you will need access to public, randomly released test items and you will need to use textbooks and other primary instructional materials. If you have already identified the knowledge, vocabulary, and skills necessary to successfully answer the questions and if you have identified the distracters in the items, all the better.

This step begins by reviewing the text and supplementary materials to check for both content and context alignment. Remember that *content alignment* refers to whether there is a match between the content covered in the test item and the instructional materials. *Context alignment* refers to whether the format of the instructional material is aligned with the test item. For each test item presented, instructional materials are reviewed to identify where there are matches and mismatches. The form in figure 4-5 could be used for this purpose.

Share material that has been developed, and determine how these materials might best be utilized. Although this activity is essential for classroom teachers interested in moving toward deep alignment, it is crucial for teachers involved in any form of special education, remediation, or re-teaching. It has been our experience that there tends to be an overreliance on the utilization of worksheets as the mechanism for remediating deficiencies among students. There are no data to suggest that this sort of remediation leads to consistent gains in student achievement. Students do respond well to material that is motivating, geared to their ability level, and enables them to be successful. Because no publisher can know the interests and ability level of the students in every class, there is no getting around the need for teachers to modify these materials and use them in ways that meet the needs and interests of the students at hand. It is called *good teaching*.

Figure 4.5   Textbook/Test Item Alignment

	Match		*Match*	
Content	*Content*	*Content*	*Content*

Presciption-Write a prescription for how the instructional materials need to be modified to achieve both content and context alignment.

Classroom Activity-Design a classroom activity that a classroom teacher could use to teach a lesson that includes instruction for both content and context alignment.

Step 6: Written Curriculum—Test Alignment

After a number of public randomly released test items have been disaggregated to identify the vocabulary, knowledge, and skills necessary for successfully answering the test items, it is time to look seriously at the existing written curriculum to see if the pre-skills leading to high student achievement are presently in the written curriculum. New learning is hard. It is not possible for students to learn all the pre-skills they need for doing well on tests during the six or seven months prior to the test. Often, the first time students take a high-stakes test is at the fourth-grade level. We recommend that students should reach mastery level of the skills assessed at the fourth grade by the end of the third grade. This gives the fourth-grade teacher an opportunity to review both the content and context of the assessment and, more importantly, engage in deep-alignment activities. If the written curriculum of the district does not reflect the expectation of mastery level achievement of the skills assessed in fourth grade by the end of third grade, the curriculum should be revised so that teachers in grades kindergarten through third grade are aware of these expectations and plan instruction to achieve this level of mastery.

It has been our experience that teachers at grade levels not assessed by high-stakes accountability measures may not understand their obligation to assure student mastery. Figure 4-6 provides a hypothetical example. In this example, it is clear that one test item at the fourth grade is actually sampling much prior learning in previous grades. Much of the kindergarten curriculum is being assessed at the fourth grade, and perhaps less with each subsequent grade. One way to ensure that teachers do understand this requirement is to make sure the necessary pre-skills are clearly stated in the written curriculum and that informal assessments are conducted at each grade level to be sure that students are achieving mastery. We caution read-

Figure 4.6   A Single Test Item's Utilization of Prior Learning

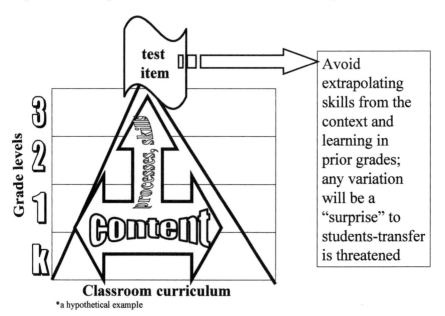

Classroom curriculum

*a hypothetical example

ers to avoid simply taking the released test items and extrapolating the skills and then reducing them to drill sheets. This kind of rote learning is not helpful for students when the test context is shifting. Rote learning only works if the test also assesses only rote learning. Once students have to place the skills into a variety of test contexts, application is being assessed; in order to avoid surprising students, application *must* be taught (see Phye, 1997, pp. 49–51).

The necessity to teach application is classroom intrusive; that is, it becomes a meta-criterion that defines the nature of the activity. Teachers are generally not accustomed to this level of prescriptive guideline. We believe that with appropriate staff development, this attitude will change. We have seen it change when teachers understand that their failure to be responsive places their children at risk of not doing well, and one consequence is that they may be punished in a variety of ways. Teachers too may be unfairly judged, especially if pupil performance is tied to their salaries. Although we are opposed to this trend, the alternative (ignoring the emerging requirements) has been made increasingly odious politically.

Currently, only one state in this union does not have state standards and that is the state of Iowa. In Iowa, each district is required by the state to establish its own standards and choose an assessment system that provides the community, state legislators, and the federal government with evidence that increasing numbers of students are achieving the standards. Most districts in the state have developed standards that mirror many state frameworks. At the same time, a large number have chosen the Iowa Test of Basic Skills (ITBS) as the measure of accountability. In most cases, the accountability assessment does not match the district-identified standards. The situation in Iowa is no different from many districts across the nation where the state assessment system is not aligned with state framework. Most states are working diligently to bring this alignment into place. The most successful states are ones that are developing or using criterion-referenced tests for the state assessment system. Those states that have adopted a national norm-referenced test, draped in secrecy, as the state accountability measure, are the ones that present the most difficult challenge to educators.

Disaggregating public, randomly released test items while aligning the written curriculum of the district to ensure that mastery of pre-skills is achieved is one way to address this difficult problem. Without this approach, teachers of grade levels where the tests are administered are often placed in a lose–lose situation because students come to their classes without the prerequisite skills and there is simply not enough instructional time to bring them to mastery.

Step 7: Going Deeper: Anticipating Where the Test is Moving

No state test is static; all assessments are changing. Even a review of standardized, norm-referenced tests over time reveals that these tests are changing and generally becoming more difficult. For example, the SAT and ACT are adding more open-ended response items to their batteries. The Terra Nova requires a higher level of critical thinking than the CTBS did twenty years ago. The state of Texas is a prime example of a state where the current state criterion-referenced test is outdated the year it is given because the test is continually being rewritten to include more difficult items.

In the case of Texas, if a teacher did everything we have suggested so far, there is no guarantee that her/his students would not be surprised when taking the next state assessment. Consequently, it is imperative that teachers anticipate the direction the test is moving and prepare students for the next iteration of the test. For example, if a state assessment system currently relies solely on multiple-choice tests, but next year students will be required to respond to a set of four open-ended response items, teachers need to be aware of the anticipated changes and include instruction this year that goes beyond the present content and context of the test.

To apply this concept, it is necessary for district administrators to cultivate open lines of communication with the state department so that these anticipated changes are known in advance. District administrators must then inform classroom teachers about the direction the test is moving and provide them with the time necessary to modify current instructional practices to accommodate the anticipated changes.

Often, teachers feel overwhelmed just keeping up with the present, let alone anticipating the future. Without accepting that things will change and attempting to anticipate what the changes will be, teachers feel that the state is playing games with them and never providing them with a clear target for what they are expected to do.

To anticipate the future direction of the test, let us assume that the same content will be used with future tests, but the format of the tests will change. It is also highly likely that the level of critical thinking required will include higher levels of *Bloom's Taxonomy, Cognitive Domain* (1956). Rather than asking questions requiring simple recall or identification of correct information, the items will ask students to synthesize information and use that information to make a determination. Teachers should be given practice taking existing released test items and making them more difficult both in context and level of critical thinking.

We believe that the concept of deep alignment is entirely consonant with what testing experts advocate about ethical and prudent test preparation practices (see Miyasaka, 2000). The test, any test, should be no big deal because alignment is an ongoing concept in good classroom instructional practice. Thus, by incorporating deep alignment into ongoing classroom teaching, we avoid all the unsavory shortcuts such as intensive, short-term test prep exercises, undue attention to the whole testing scenario, scaring children half to death about the "big bad test," and resorting to drill and kill ditto sheet and workbook boredom.

Figure 4-7 shows how to create pedagogical parallelism with deep alignment in three steps. Step 1 is to obtain and then deconstruct a public, randomly released test item and establish a comparable classroom environment/activity that includes the concepts, skills, and knowledge. Step 2 is to engage in the first tweak by expanding beyond what the item is assessing and include some different methods of assessing it. Step 3 is to go much further beyond the concepts, knowledge, and processes by using a variety of assessment approaches. The item is still embedded in the activity, but it is becoming a smaller and smaller aspect of the classroom environment or activity. In this way, the teacher assures the children that they will not be

Figure 4.7   Creating Deep Classroom Curriculum Alignment with Pedagogical Parallelism

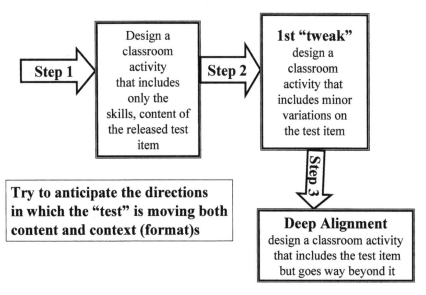

surprised by either the content or the context of any item on the test. In this situation, the content has been greatly expanded to include the full content domain, and a full array of possible test formats has been experienced as an ongoing aspect of classroom instruction.

One of the problems in classroom teaching has been that both formative and summative evaluation practices have not been taught to prospective teachers to any great depth, if at all, in their teacher education programs. Classroom evaluation practices have been notoriously poor and unreliable (see Popham, 1981, pp. 46–47). Our experience with staff development programs covering deep alignment has convinced most teachers that good teaching means preparing one's students to handle any form of assessment so that they are not surprised. This is the only fair way to really ascertain what they have learned. To do so means becoming conversant with the way tests work.

KEY CONCEPTS OF THIS CHAPTER

Conceptual scaffolding   The intrinsic structure that exists within specific curriculum areas comprising its essential elements, strands, big ideas, or core knowledge

Content   The essence of a curriculum area that can be expressed as core knowledge, ideas, themes, big ideas, or essential factual nuggets

Context   The format or situation in which knowledge may be presented and or tested

Deep alignment   The concept that what is tested is contained in what is taught, but that what is taught is not confined to the test. Teaching that is engaged in deep alignment is anticipating ways of assessment in which important information, concepts, processes, or dispositions may be tested.

Pedagogical parallelism   Classrooms can be set up so that specific testing approaches are embedded in activities, which children undertake, but which are not exclusively confined to them. The idea is that children should be afforded an opportunity to practice what and how they may be assessed on high-stakes measures of accountability prior to being tested. An extrapolation of the idea of the transfer of learning in identical situations.

The teachable moment   A point in classroom instruction where the interests of children become the focal point of teaching, as opposed to the curriculum. It is often a place where the teacher is presented with an opportunity to reinforce prior learning in a serendipitous manner.

APPLICATIONS

1. Creating an Alignment Resource Packet

Purpose: To be sure everyone in the system understands the meaning of deep alignment.

In order to be sure that everyone in the system has a common vocabulary for discussing issues related to deep alignment, a resource packet should be developed by central administrative staff and placed in each building's professional development library. This packet should contain a glossary of terms, relevant journal articles, and examples of materials produced for each of the steps recommended in this chapter. These examples should relate to primary instructional materials and district-wide assessments for each grade and content area assessed. Each time new primary instructional materials are purchased, the resource packet should be updated so that teachers always have ready access to information necessary to engage in deep alignment.

2. Creating Professional Development Modules

Purpose: To be sure all staff has the information necessary to implement deep alignment practices in classrooms.

Initially, professional development activities should be developed for everyone in the system. This includes newly hired teachers, supervisors, building administrators, and master teachers. The concept of deep alignment is relatively new in the literature. To be sure that everyone understands the concept, a series of professional development sessions should be planned for each group. These activities should be fashioned around the role of the persons attending. For instance, building administrators will benefit from focusing on how to determine that deep alignment practices are being utilized by classroom teachers. This will require that principals become proficient in conducting classroom observations to determine the degree of planning for deep alignment that has taken place and the success of these efforts. A principal displaying this level of sophistication will have to be knowledgeable about the written curriculum and the primary instructional materials available to staff for implementing the curriculum. This principal will have to be thoroughly familiar with the district/state assessment system and aware of both the context and content assessed. In addition, he/she will have to possess a comprehensive knowledge of a wide array of the types of assessment. It will not be sufficient for the principal to simply be familiar with the context of the present assessment tool used by the district or the state. This principal will also have to have a thorough understanding of alternative assessment measures. This knowledge should be at a level sufficient for the principal to provide teachers with suggestions of implementing a wide variety of alternative assessments.

Newly hired teachers are another group that needs intensive professional development about deep alignment. It is almost certain that this concept was not part of their preparation program, since it has only recently emerged as part of the accountability movement. The professional development offered to these teachers provides an excellent opportunity for district administrators to set high expectations for classroom instructional practices. By insisting that all teachers in the system are expected to engage in deep alignment, new teachers are more likely to try to meet this standard and seek assistance from mentors, supervisors, and principals if they need help, and they will need help.

Administrators may find that the best teachers in the district are already employing these practices. By insisting that newly hired teachers meet this standard too, the number of teachers employing these practices will grow each year. Because of this, other teachers are more likely to expand their skills in planning for deep alignment. This is especially true when central office and building administrators insist that implementing deep alignment practices is a district, school, and classroom goal for every teacher in the system.

It is possible to dramatically change classroom practices with such a focused effort. We would argue that student achievement results would be higher with this effort than from adopting a new program.

3. Identifying an Alignment Mentor in Each Building

Purpose: To provide an on-site contact as a resource for expanding deep alignment practices.

Knowing that there is someone on staff who can answer questions about deep alignment can be quite instrumental in facilitating the implementation of these practices. This individual would have to be provided with enough release time to act as a coach to classroom teachers. With the present trend toward inclusion, this teacher may be part of the special education faculty, Title I, or other staff with assigned remediation duties. This person would have to receive specialized training in deep alignment techniques and feel comfortable acting as a support person to other faculty.

As teachers become more proficient in implementing deep alignment techniques, the mentor could be responsible for the identification of exemplary practices being implemented at the building and finding ways to inform the rest of the staff about these practices. This could lead to an annual deep alignment showcase where identified teachers explain their practices to a wider audience.

The deep alignment mentor would also be responsible for developing and delivering awareness sessions for parents and other stakeholders. As parents continue to become more savvy about effective instructional practices, they too may want to engage in these activities at home.

4. Developing Action Research Projects

Purpose: To document the effectiveness of these practices for improving student achievement.

Invite teachers to apply for small stipends to support action research efforts dealing with deep alignment. Offer teachers a $200 grant to support the effort. Teachers would have to complete a proposal that included a statement of the problem, a description of the deep alignment activities to be implemented, a mechanism for collecting both formative and summative data, and a description of the criteria used to determine the effectiveness of the strategies. Over time, this effort could produce a rich database of effective deep alignment practices. These studies could lead to conference presentations and written articles.

REFERENCES

Bloom, B., Englehart, M., Furst, E., Hill, W., and Krathwohl, D. (1956). *Taxonomy of educational objectives: Handbook 1 cognitive domain.* New York: David McKay.

Bolster, L. (1991). *Exploring mathematics grade 7.* Glenview, IL: Scott Foresman.

Boser, U. (2000, March 8). States face limited choices in assessment market. *Education Week* 29 (26), 1–22.

Bright, E. (1992). Teachers' views of ethical standardized test use. Paper presented at the annual meeting of the National Council on Measurement in Education, San Francisco, CA, April. ERIC, ED 347 168.

Chang, S. and Raths, J. (1971). The school's contribution to the cumulating deficit. *Journal of Educational Research* 64, 272.

Cohen, S., and Hyman, J. (1991, Spring). Can fantasies become facts? *Educational Measurement: Issues and Practice,* 20–23, citing S. Cohen et al., Comparing effects of meta-cognitive learning styles and human attributes with alignment.

Paper given at the American Education Research Association (1989). San Francisco, CA.

Comer, L. and Keeves, J. (1973). *Science education in nineteen countries: International studies in evaluation.* New York: Wiley.

Crowell, R., and Tissot, P. (1986). *Curriculum alignment*, Oak Brook, IL: North Central Regional Educational Laboratory. ERIC, ED 280 874.

Freeman, D., and Porter, P. (1988). Does the content of classroom instruction match the content of textbooks? Paper presented the 'American Education Association, New Orleans, LA.

Gamoran, A., Porter, A., Smithson, J., and White, P. (1997, Winter). Upgrading high school mathematics instruction: Improving learning opportunities for low-achieving, low-income youth. *Educational Evaluation and Policy Analysis* 19 (4), 325–338.

Husen, T. (1967). *International study of achievement in mathematics: A comparison of twelve countries*, vol.2. New York: Wiley.

Lynch, K. (1990). An evaluation of curriculum alignment as a process of improving academic achievement (effective schools). Ed.D. dissertation, University of La Verne, CA.

McNeil, L. (2000, June). Creating new inequalities: Contradictions of reform. *Phi Delta Kappan* 81 (10), 728–736.

Moss-Mitchell, F. (1998, May). The effects of curriculum alignment on the mathematics achievement of third-grade students as measured by the Iowa Test of Basic Skills: Implications for educational administrators. Unpublished doctoral dissertation, Clark University.

Miyasaka, J. (2000). A framework for evaluating the validity of test preparation practices. Unpublished paper, American Education Research Association, New Orleans, LA.

Phye, G. (1997). Classroom assessment: A multidimensional approach. In G. Phye (ed.) *Handbook of classroom assessment*. San Diego, CA: Academic, 33–51.

Pogrow, S. (1999, November). Rejoinder: Consistent large gains and high levels of achievement are the best measures of program quality: Pogrow responds to Slavin. *Educational Researcher* 28 (8), 24–27.

Popham, J. (1981). *Modern educational measurement*. Englewood Cliffs, NJ: Prentice Hall.

Price-Baugh, R. (1997). Correlation of textbook alignment with student achievement scores. Unpublished doctoral dissertation, Baylor University.

Stevens, F. (1984). *The effects of testing on teaching and curriculum in a large urban school district*. Washington, DC: National Institute of Education. Report No. ERIC-TM-88. 8 ERIC, ED 252 581.

Thorndike, E. (1913). The psychology of learning. *Educational Psychology* 2. New York: Columbia University Press.

Whithead, A. (1959). *The aims of education and other essays.* New York: Macmillan.

Zellmer, M. (1997). Effect on reading test scores when teachers are provided information that relates local curriculum documents to the test. Unpublished doctoral dissertation, Marquette University.

Creating a Viable Alternative to Testing as Mass Inspection

Teachers and principals often look back to the times prior to high-stakes testing and remember them as idyllic, even pastoral. There was a time when tests were not all that important, and teaching and learning seemed much more fun (Steinberg, 2000, p. 16). We doubt those days will ever return to public education. We do think the nature of testing will change, and we believe that the conditions requiring such changes are already becoming apparent (see Kohn, 2000).

The purpose of this chapter is to sketch out a more balanced perspective on testing than currently exists in the United States. We see the current period as one in which the respective states are exerting their political control and dominance over school curricula via testing as becoming a permanent fixture, even as the forms of testing are being altered.

PROBLEMS WITH CURRENT FORMS OF HIGH-STAKES ACCOUNTABILITY TESTING

Currently, the problems with state-centered forms of high-stakes testing are:

- Too many are dominated by norm-referenced, standardized tests, which measure no specific curriculum, and consequently provide very little useful information for teachers and principals to actually change classroom practice (see Neill, 2000);
- The range of the curriculum assessed by current tests is too limited (not very broad) and not very deep (Schmidt, McKnight, and Raizen, 1996; Neill, 2000, p. 32);

- The political context of testing is punitive, negative, and destructive of teacher initiative and creativity, and falls outside the curricular boundaries of the tested curriculum (see Kohn, 2000). Research by Firestone, Fitz, and Broadfoot (1999) showed that centralized assessment practices failed to stimulate constructivist teaching (p. 788). Testing programs in some countries are designed to alarm the public about the deficiencies in the schools and are aimed at undermining support for public schools in order to reduce expenditures for education (see Carnoy, 1999, p. 61) and bear a remarkable resemblance to current political rhetoric in the U.S. (Reich, 2000, p. 26);
- The use of statewide testing falsely rewards most school districts, which are already serving privileged pupil populations because such instruments are highly sensitive to measures of wealth and other nonschool-controlled demographic factors (see Carnoy, 1999, p. 29; Wilkins, 2000);
- The use of current tests rewards the memorization and utilization of inert information, which is antithetical to the wide range of diverse student intellectual and artistic interests, which are present in nearly all student bodies today;
- The overall impact of high-stakes testing on school curricula is one of relentless reductionism leading to an absurd form of values about learning; that is, if it isn't tested, it isn't worth learning because it doesn't count for anything (see DuBois, Eaton, Garet, and Miller, 2000);
- The implementation of a variety of salary schemes to pay teachers and/or principals for performance is highly reminiscent of Frederick Taylor's piece-rate system approach which became known as *scientific management* (Kanigel, 1997, p. 230). It is based on dubious assumptions regarding singular and linear expressions of job-related tasks and learning results obtained. Such salary approaches debase both teaching and learning because they oversimplify what occurs within each and create the conditions for a continuation of simplistic forms of measurement, particularly the extension of norm-referenced, standardized tests (Sacks, 1999). We recount here the experience of educational reform in Kentucky (Steffy, 1993). Where once the state led the nation in the use of alternative forms of measurement that emphasized the higher-level thinking skills, the insistence on using the data to support rewards and sanctions (such as performance pay) and state intervention exposed the alternative forms to the fact that they were not reliable enough. Reliability is part of the way the older tests defined themselves. The fact that reliability (defined as consistency) and inflexibility are interrelated

should be obvious. Alternative forms of assessment may not be as reliable, but that may have to be sacrificed when more important educational aims are at stake. Yet due-process specifications must prevail when dollars are to be related to results. We doubt that the Kentucky assessment system would have been scrapped if rewards and sanctions had not been a part of it. The re-adoption of more traditional assessment tests in Kentucky was a step backward from the bold initiatives that once propelled this imaginative approach to educational reform.

On the other hand, we are firm believers in measurement as an integral part of the teaching/learning process. We generally support the creation of standards of learning when they are not reductionistic and part of an overall strategy to reduce state expenditures for public education, which further polarizes children into the socio-economic higher and lower classes of the nation (see Carnoy, 1999, p. 30; Fiske and Ladd, 2000, p. 38).

POSITIVE TRENDS IN STATE ASSESSMENT PROGRAMS

These are the trends that we support in positive assessment programs:

Toward Forms of Assessment That Follow Curricular Initiatives and Do Not Define or Become Surrogates for Them

Assessment programs should not drive educational reform—they should follow it. The selection of the forms of assessment should be predicated on the kinds of curricular reforms that are desired. The curriculum should define the nature of education and schooling rather than being held hostage to the assessment process.

We believe that a broad-based program of curricular reform should be jointly initiated at the national and state levels, and that the U.S. Department of Education should establish the requirements for assessment which are first and foremost measures of a specific curriculum which is held to be common for the entire country.

Toward Not Driving Curricular or Educational Standards with High-Stakes Assessment Programs That Debase the Very Changes They Are Designed to Measure

We believe that driving educational reform with assessment is bad practice because it substitutes the process of assessment with the main business of schooling that is teaching and learning. One does not come to school to be assessed, but to engage in teaching and learning. Assessment is the means to determine if teaching and learning have been effective; it should not be a substitute for it. When the tests themselves become the basis for determining whether a reform has worked or not, we have substituted the measurement for that which it was ostensibly designed to measure (see Penniman, 2000).

Toward Curriculum-Centered Assessment That Is Open and Public

The best form of assessment occurs when it is deeply aligned with the curriculum. There is no need for secrecy because the curriculum to be assessed is open and public. This condition applies in England and Wales, where each year's national test is made public, but not in the states (see Firestone, Fitz, and Broadfoot, 1999, p. 770). In an open atmosphere, testing contents have been demystified. Practice tests are publicly available on the Internet and in forms for parents to read and understand (also see Claycomb and Kysilko, 2000). One result is that in England and Wales, curriculum alignment is a routine practice, but not in the United States (Firestone, Fitz, and Broadfoot, 1999, pp. 775, 778). Recently, U.S. educational leaders have begun to call for making the tests public (see Musick, 2000, p. 84).

Toward J Curves Instead of Bell Curves

The frequency distribution known as the *bell curve* has been replaced with *the J curve*, a distribution based on mastery in which schooling and the processes of education are not considered random variables. *J curves* mean that as the curricular standards are made public, most children are going to be able to exhibit mastery of them. No test is considered inappropriate because too many children are passing. The so-called rigor of a test is not going to be determined by the number of children who fail to pass it.

Toward Curricular Inclusivity and Multiculturalism

We embrace the view that curriculum, especially that which is concerned with creating a national polity, becomes culturally inclusive, rather than exclusive, and we recognize that the concept of inclusivity is itself a construction of power with a discourse about power (see Popkewitz, 2000, p. 22). America has always been a diverse country and has become more diverse over time. But the "color line" that was the most pressing social problem of the last century remains the most pressing problem of the twenty-first. America's social policy for minorities has included a checkered past of slavery (Osofsky, 1967; Jordan, 1968; Davis, 1975); land invasion/removal and genocide for Native Americans; cheap labor and national exclusion acts for Asians (Daniels, 1974; Chen, 1980), which later manifested itself in the creation of concentration camps for Japanese-Americans based solely on their race (Bosworth, 1967); and colonization and land theft from Hispanics (Carter, 1970; Servin 1974; Mirande and Enriquez, 1979; Montejano, 1987). American public schools have utilized institutionalized forms of exclusion, deprivation, and punishment as part and parcel of their internal operations based on a person's skin color, religion, or national origin (Tyack, 1974, pp. 110–125, 217–229; Kluger, 1975). The so-called melting pot only worked if a person erased all forms of his/her cultural heritage; for persons of color, they were exposed to continuing discrimination because of their inability to "melt" (Donaldson and Seepe, 1999, p. 331).

As the overt forms of institutionalized racism have come under attack and been legally eliminated, the schools are left with vestiges of them. Attitudes are harder to erase. The lack of expectation that children of color can learn or are not genetically impaired is still rampant in too many schools designed to serve them. Indeed, they are not served at all; they are subjugated into a socially and economically inferior position (Lynch, 1999). As one example, we point out here the American Civil Liberty Union's suit in California about the lack of the availability of AP (Advanced Placement) classes for African American and Latino students (Glasser, 2000, p. 2). Access to AP classes, which places a student in a privileged position to get into a highly competitive California university, has become even more crucial since the California electorate abolished affirmative action in 1996. That vote dropped the number of African American students at the Berkeley campus by 50 percent and the number of Latino students by over 40 percent (Glasser, 2000, p. 2).

Multiculturalism means not only dealing with inequalities based on race, gender, disability, and sexual orientation, but social class (Sleeter and Grant, 1988). It is in the matter of social class that the underlying economic disparities of life come to the forefront. From the very beginning of I.Q. testing, social class has mattered in terms of higher scores linked to greater wealth, even as the experts express a lack of understanding as to the causes (see Jensen, 1980, pp. 367–368). Matters of social class inequities bridge the concern with forming a curriculum that is not only inclusive for diverse cultures, but one that is shaped to deal with matters of social and economic justice in the larger society. We are encouraged by some explorations in social justice that deal with the concept of social capital as a vehicle to raise student aspirations and provide an environment for academic learning (see Kahne and Bailey, 1999, p. 322).

Toward Education for Social and Economic Justice

At the root of the chasm that separates the *haves* from the *have-nots* is an economical–political system that spawns greed, privilege, and domination masked as principles of liberty and support for individual initiative. Such a worldwide system has produced a situation in which the "assets of the world's leading 358 billionaires exceed the combined annual incomes of approximately half the population of the globe" (McLaren, 1997, p. 3). A recent World Bank study of growing worldwide income disparity noted, "The distribution of these gains [in prosperity] is extraordinarily unequal" (Phillips, 2000, p. A2).

A curriculum that deals with social justice will include examples of historical and continuing racism and economic oppression. Teaching students how to engage in nonviolent and constructive social change begins with illustrating how the economic system works to find the cheapest labor markets to produce goods. One example is the maquiladoras, the 4000 factories and firms that in Mexico employ one million workers producing "value-added goods" worth more than $7 billion per year (*The Economist,* 1998, p. 13). Corporate giants such as Sony, Hitachi, Sanyo, Samsung, and Hyundai pay Mexican workers one-fifth of what workers in the U.S. would receive (*The Economist,* 1998, p. 14).

There are two approaches to addressing social justice issues in school curriculum. They are: (1) the accommodationist approach for gradualistic change based on social action over time, and (2) the social empowerment approach that may involve nonviolent but confrontational tactics in the larger public socioeconomic spheres. The latter course is the most dangerous for state-supported schools that are dependent on public taxes for their existence. Students from well-to-do families will have vocal parents who will be loath to have their children learn about and engage in activities aimed at changing the social class structure. Such parents see the schools as places to maintain and advance their own social class standing in an economically competitive society (see Sapon-Shevin, 1994, pp. 204–216).

The accommodationist model is one of maintenance of subcultural groups while at the same time "assuming their overall acculturation to the dominate culture" (LaBelle and Ward, 1994, p. 167). In this model, dominant societal members become sensitive to the viewpoints and perspectives of minorities, developing respect for their right to be different. However, such a curriculum eschews radical social confrontation to change economic injustice where it may be present.

The social empowerment approach develops activist citizens as its goal, citizens who are not afraid to engage in nonviolent protest to change unjust economic conditions. We think of the grape boycott lead by Cesar Chavez in California (Levy, 1975). Although farm workers engaged in picketing were repeatedly brutalized and attacked by the owners and their thugs while police stood by and watched (Matthiessen, 1969, p. 85), millions of American citizens sympathetic to Chavez boycotted California grapes. Holding the strikers up as persons engaging in positive participation in developing a more socially just and fairer economic society has always been dangerous for teachers and administrators in the public schools. There are those critics of such a curriculum that the school should teach just the facts without endeavoring to instill the values that lie behind them. Although such a value-free curriculum does not exist anywhere, there are members of the public and boards of education who naively believe such a situation is possible. It is also extremely difficult for the schools to try and produce changes in the larger socioeconomic scene when business leaders, whose main motive is efficiency, are held up as models for school administrators to emulate (see Callahan, 1962). Such a situation continues into present times because of the vulnerability of the superintendency to community/legislative pressures (see Eaton, 1990).

REASSERTING THE PRIMACY OF CURRICULUM IN THE TESTING DEBATE

We attribute the misuse and abuse of testing in the U.S. to false scientism of so-called objective assessment, which has been shown to be a myth (Fine, 1975; Purvin, 1977; Cole, 1977; Owen, 1985), and political efforts by a variety of groups trying to avoid a national curriculum (see Manatt, 1995). The obsession of many Americans with federal direction and control has worked to handicap efforts to come to grips with the lack of a truly national curriculum. Such a system would define the nature of the desired learning considered essential for all Americans. We endorse the current efforts to develop national standards (see Tucker and Codding, 1998), but these cannot be considered a national curriculum.

There are at least two major problems in developing a national curriculum, apart from the paranoia of some local curricular diehards opposed to expanding federal control under any aegis. We are aware that a significant number of persons of many stripes simply mistrust government in any form (see Reinhart, 1999, pp. 15–16). The problems with determining a national curriculum are not unique to the United States. The former Soviet Union became so perplexed about what curriculum to teach that graduate exams in history were cancelled in 1991 (Lisovskaya, 1999, p. 210).

In Japan, national history has for many years excluded any precise accounting of that nation's aggressions in World War II in their textbooks (Nash, Crabtree, and Dunn, 1997, pp. 134–135). Such blatant Japanese practices as forcing Korean women to become "comfort females" to Japanese troops is not a textbook topic, nor was the practice of forcing Chinese men to become slave laborers in Japan and work in the coal mines for some of the most famous Japanese companies today, namely Mitsui and the Mitsubishi Corporation (Forney, 2000, p. A19).

In 1988, the English Parliament adopted a National Curriculum that aroused great controversy. In history, what "got in" to the National Curriculum were "Victorian Britain and the American Revolution. But others—the Protestant Reformation, World War I, the Holocaust, and the history of Ireland—did not get in" (Nash, Crabtree, and Dunn, 1997, p. 141). In addition, no social history about Britain's expanding racial and ethnic minorities was included.

Australia still struggles to reconcile its history and the oppression of the Aborigine peoples, who into the 1960s could not vote, were denied citizenship, and were not even counted in the Australian census (Brooks and Horwitz, 2000, p. A1). Because groups are competing with one another socially and economically, it has been the wielding of political power that has resolved issues such as "Whose history, science, or literature shall be taught?" The political right in the United States has a fear of diversity. It fears its influence will be lost with growing minority populations. The key to that influence is in the white male identity. The idea of multiculturalism is anathema. It is portrayed as divisive to national unity in exactly the same way current white Australians fear that a public apology to the Aborigines would "escalate demands for compensation and further divide Australia" (Brooks and Horwitz, 2000, p. A1). When Lynne Cheney, then former chairman of the National Endowment for the Humanities, blasted the new history standards in *The Wall Street Journal* (1994) because of their gloomy portrayal of past American problems, it was quickly followed by right-wing radio darling Rush Limbaugh who falsely accused academics who had worked on the history standards as engaging in indoctrination that "our country is inherently evil" (Nash, Crabtree, and Dunn, 1997, p. 5). Limbaugh urged his listeners that the new history standards should be flushed "down the sewer of multiculturalism" (Nash, Crabtree, and Dunn, 1997, p. 5).

Political control of education in the United States has been in the hands of the respective states and they have moved to enhance their power base (see Adams and Kirst, 1999, p. 485). We are suggesting that this movement has impeded the development of a truly national curriculum. A national curriculum would stand as a bulwark to the peculiar idiosyncrasies that develop from time to time at the state level. We think here of the Kansas State Board of Education, which took a curriculum developed by science experts and turned it over to "a local group of creationists for revision" (Baringer, 2000, p. A27). The result was the elimination of evolution, the Big Bang theory, and geologic time because it was perceived that they conflicted with Biblical text, notably Genesis. We believe that the states' control over curriculum, in which each individual state's history becomes part of curricular requirements, is obsolete. There is nothing in North Dakota, North Carolina, or Alabama state histories that has anything to do with international comparability on important educational standards. It is time for the development of a truly national educational curriculum, which represents the best thinking in every discipline, and which is comparable to the nations of the world with which America desires to be judged.

The resolution of one peculiar problem is important to this idea and that concerns the separation of church and state. A key to this development is that as far as the public schools are concerned, all religions are equal in development of policies of civil toleration (see Douglas, 1966). Bates (1993) defines *civil toleration* as meaning equality in the eyes of the state (p. 311). Some parents reject this stance as being the equivalent of their religious beliefs being equal spiritually, which by their own religious choices they have outright rejected. We believe that although the schools can teach about religion, the curriculum ought not to be shaped by any one specific religious viewpoint. Because nearly all of the rulings regarding the separation of church and state have involved the U.S. Supreme Court as the ultimate arbiter, that religious freedom—as well as freedom from any specific religious doctrine—is best ensured by the federal government from the perspective of the United States Constitution. Many state legislatures and agencies have permitted abuses in the area of church/state relationships in the past. In fact, the state, in the area of school segregation, stood as a major obstacle to the implementation of equal schooling for all children, regardless of their race, for many decades (see Kluger, 1975). Only the national anvil of a national curriculum can deal with the pressures applied to state legislatures in which they have compromised basic U.S. Constitutional guarantees to students in the past. For these reasons, we believe it is time to take steps to create a national curriculum benchmarked to national and international standards of excellence.

We see the creation of a national curriculum as a necessary and crucial first step in moving toward any form of true national assessment. A national curriculum is also crucial in order to reverse the practice of testing first and devising a curriculum second. For any test to be valuable to classroom teachers, it must be assessing what they have been hired to teach, in whole or in part.

We see plenty of room for local and state initiatives in a national curriculum. We do not envision a national curriculum as so dominant as to permit no state or local inclusions of curriculum. However, we decry local or state initiatives that insist on adding peculiarities that have no value outside the assumption that they are merely local or state. Specifically, we believe that any state's history should be eliminated as a requirement in the social studies curriculum, and that creationism should not be part of the science curriculum. Creationism is not science; it is faith. Science and scientific theories invite refutation as a matter of course (see Popper, 1968). Creationism is neither a theory, nor does it seek refutation (see Numbers, 1992). We have no objection to creationism being taught in a course dealing with religions of the world, or a course in philosophy, or even in a class about contemporary thought in U.S. society, but creationism has no place in science.

We see the best minds in America devising a national curriculum that is scientifically accurate, rigorous, and comparable to the most exacting international benchmarks available. The children of America are children of the world, and a global society requires a global education. The curriculum for a global education cannot be confined to Arkansas or even New York, and it is certainly beyond any local education agency's purview or expertise to create. If the people of America want an accurate measure of the merits of public education, there should be a truly national curriculum that is being assessed in such a test. Such a curriculum does not now exist and it is unlikely to exist even with the adoption of national standards. Standards are the guides for developing a curriculum; they are not a curriculum in themselves.

In reviewing the requirements for an education that truly prepares students for a global economy, Carnoy (1999) comments that, "Because knowledge is the most highly valued commodity in the global economy, nations have little choice but to increase their investment in education" (p. 82). Carnoy also stipulates that there is no evidence that some of the popular reforms being advocated about improving educational quality actually work. Among those are decentralization, privatization, and parental involvement in the schools (p. 85).

THE TERRAIN OF STRUGGLE: WHAT DOES IT MEAN TO TEACH SOCIAL JUSTICE?

Teaching social justice in schools means awakening students to the inequities and social injustices that are present in America and in the world.

Social justice is not some abstract idea, but a reality in a world in which "some 1.2 billion people live on less than $1 a day, with 2.8 billion, almost half the planet's population, surviving on a daily income of less than $2" (Phillips, 2000, p. A2). These data are derived from a study conducted by the World Bank, which concluded, "In a world where political power is unequally distributed and often mimics the distribution of economic power, the way state institutions operate may be particularly unfavorable to poor people" (Phillips, 2000, p. A2).

No society is perfect. America is not an exception. There are faults with America as any other country in the world. The meaning of America is redefined and revised with each generation. Laws succeed earlier laws. Where once slavery was legal, now it is not. Where once racial discrimination was permitted on trains and in public schools, now it is not. So there is plenty of evidence that the definition of America was not perfect in the first place. To admit to such imperfections is not an indulgence in denigration or an admission that somehow America "is evil," as portrayed by Rush Limbaugh or Lynne Cheney in their past castigation of the new history standards (Nash, Crabtree, and Dunn, 1997, pp. 3-5). The greatness of America lies in the efforts of its citizens to make it a better, more tolerant and inclusive place than its history demonstrates.

In approaching teaching social justice in the schools, the social empowerment model offers a promising approach to changing American society to become more sensitive, tolerant, and just. We propose the following principles as organizing themes for the social studies curriculum (see also LaBelle and Ward, 1994, pp. 169–170):

- Reflecting on current life circumstances
- Learning social action skills
- Practicing democratic social activism
- Learning to construct action coalitions
- Engaging in democratic social change

For social justice to come alive in the classroom, the central aspect of becoming a reality is the understanding of the classroom teacher that he/she is working in a terrain of struggle (Darder, 1991, p. 102). Such a terrain represents a contested foci for students and teachers. Few teachers have been prepared to engage in critical reflection that calls into question their own worldview and the source of their authority. Without confronting the social class chasm in U.S. society, the teacher may become a "pseudo-critical educator" who talks about empowering students, but actually is only strengthening his or her own position of authority in a system in which teachers are held captive (Darder, 1991, p. 176).

Power and hegemony not only dominate the larger society, but are represented and reproduced unconsciously in classrooms (Gramsci, 1971; Giroux, 1997). "In other words, students and teachers assume that the way school functions and the relationships inherent in school structures are un-changeable and not to be questioned" (Gutierrez and Larson, 1994, p. 22). Empirical analysis of classroom teacher/student talk reveals such structures at work, that is, where the language and culture of minority children are devalued and marginalized (Pruyn, 1994, p. 37).

The transformation of hegemonic classrooms which reinforce unequal socioeconomic conditions in the larger society means envisioning the class-room as a place of struggle for both the teacher and the students in their efforts to answer these questions:

- How are the larger cultural, economical, and political interests served by educational institutions and practices?
- Whom does education empower and whom does it disenfranchise?
- What is the role of the student in the educational system?
- What is the role of the teacher in the same system?
- What are the social functions of knowledge? (Pruyn, 1994, p. 39; Popkewitz, 2000)

These questions cut right to the center of the first organizing theme for a social empowerment curriculum, namely, reflecting current life circum-stances from a variety of perspectives.

The social empowerment model influences the reflective teacher who understands his or her own role in the existing socioeconomic system, and has a commitment to students to work with them in pursuit of their un-derstanding. As Delgado-Gaitan and Trueba (1991, p. 139) summarize:

[empowerment] starts within the self, and the place of the individual in a given society. One's own place in society cannot be surrendered. It must be defended by exercising the right to participate in the social, legal, political, and economic systems that determine individual status and his/her access to knowledge or other forms of power.

The right to fully participate in American life means engaging in law-ful activities to change socioeconomic conditions that empower some and disenfranchise others. The right to confront inequality directly, the right to protest, demonstrate, engage in boycotts, picket, and distribute and sign petitions are integral parts of engaging in social empowerment. In the end, power is not something one only talks about. Power is something that requires action. Action begins with critical reflection.

The second aspect of a social empowerment model involves learning the social action skills necessary to attain empowerment within the current socioeconomic system. These have already been described. They involve understanding how to engage in changing things, especially when the power relationships are nowhere near favorable. Students can learn how to engage in positive social change under these circumstances from the work of Gandhi (1948, p. 414), who toiled at the tasks of a teacher on his ashram or farm. If anyone was conscious of forms of power, it was Gandhi. He came to the question of how to train the spirit and in a moment of reflection wrote the following:

> the training of the spirit was possible only through the exercise of the spirit. And the exercise of the spirit entirely depended on the life and character of the teacher. . . . I saw, therefore, that I must be an eternal object-lesson to the boys and girls living with me. They thus became my teachers, and I learnt I must be good and live straight, if only for their sakes.

One sees in Gandhi's reflection his view of his relationships with students. He was not their master *over them* but a colleague in learning *with them*. One sees in Gandhi's often very critical self-analysis his deepening understanding of who he was, what he believed, and how he actually "taught" children this lesson by living with them, as opposed to telling them from a position of authority.

Another excellent source for understanding forms of social action is in the works of Saul Alinsky (1969, 1972). Alinsky understood contemporary American political power. He assisted and organized one of the most marginalized groups in Chicago and made them a force to be reckoned with. He brought the most powerful superintendent of the times to his political knees over racial segregation in the Chicago public schools (see Horwitt, 1989, pp. 405–406). Alinsky used all of the forms of social protest open to him. He had no patience with those who worked outside the system or who would destroy the system. He eschewed fixed truths, including Marxism (Alinsky, 1969, p. xii). Describing how a person would act in changing an unjust social order, Alinsky said that such an individual would be "loose, resilient, fluid, and on the move in a society which is in a state of extraordinary and constant change. He is not shackled with dogma. In our world today rigidity is fatal" (Alinsky, 1969, p. xiv). Alinsky's one abiding principle was that he professed "a belief in people, a complete commitment to the belief that if people have the power, the opportunity to act, in the long run they will, most of the time, reach the right decisions" (Alinsky, 1969, p. xiv). We think Alinsky's principles and his methods deserve a place in the classroom in the social empowerment model.

The best method to learn social activism is to practice it in the classroom and the school. Here we see more participative school environments and classrooms than normally exist. We also see students and teachers working on community-based projects that relate to matters of socioeconomic justice. A variety of projects may be open in any community, from working for better housing for the poor, to assisting poor persons to register to vote, and to enabling the poor to become eligible for whatever benefits are available to them in health and employment.

In order to accomplish some community-based projects, it will be necessary to construct coalitions of other interested parties, such as senior citizens or forum groups, which bring together the common interests of many persons. Learning how to create a coalition and maintain its viability and focus will be a crucial result of many activities.

Finally, engaging in democratic social change may take one or more of many forms such as attendance at town meetings, circulating petitions for actions, writing letters to the editor of the local newspaper, making videos or films of poverty areas and living or working conditions that should be changed, or writing a grant proposal to a public or private agency.

One of the projects of a social empowerment model is that the students and the teachers may protest having to engage in a state testing program that they perceive as anti-teacher and anti-student. In England, teachers boycotted the national assessment program on the only grounds open to them, that is, it resulted in a "massive overload caused by the new assessments" (Firestone, Fitz, and Broadfoot, 1999, p. 769). In Massachusetts, Bruce Penniman (2000), the Massachusetts Teacher of the Year for 1999, commented that the statewide testing program in the Bay State had become centered in traditional content knowledge, focused on marketplace values and centralized power. "The MCAS program has been designed to make public schools look like failures to pave the way for privatizing education" (p. 25). Penniman then set down some standards of his own regarding education reform that have been echoed in this book:

- Set broad, realistic learning standards
- Reduce the emphasis on standardized testing
- Report student performance accurately

- Provide appropriate alternatives
- Stop the cycle of blame (pp. 25–26)

Social justice cannot be taught in schools if a statewide test drives it out of the curriculum by testing only factoids, basic skills, and rote computation. Carlson (1993) notes that an emphasis on basic skills only for children of the poor may actually set them up for entry-level jobs that "solidify their subordinate position within the existent socioeconomic order" (p. 226). The latest national poll on statewide tests linked to graduation from high school, conducted by the Business Roundtable, showed that about two-thirds of the respondents favored the idea, but that "Maryland and Delaware have scaled back their test plans, and others have struggled with questions such as how high to set the passing grade and whether to test factual recall or analysis" (Kronholz, 2000, p. A2).

Testing programs must have broad-based purposes that emphasize authentic forms, which include portfolios and open-ended response items. Such forms cost more to grade and do not have the same type of reliability or validity as the standardized variety (see Haertel, 1994), yet we consider a broad-based form of assessment that emphasizes syntheses and application in multidimensional, multicultural settings as the form of national assessment.

COLLEGES OF EDUCATION: SOLUTIONS OR PROBLEMS?

Macedo (1994, p. 152) has blasted colleges of education because the most conservative faculty resides there. He defines that conservatism as follows:

> These faculties concentrate on reproducing values designed to maintain the status quo while de-skilling teachers through a labyrinth of how-to courses devoid of any substantive content. . . . Often the content ignores subordinate students' culture production and the antagonistic relations generated by the discriminating school practices and the subsequent resistance of students to 'savage inequalities.'

The training of teachers in too many colleges of education concentrates on technique, ignoring the social and cultural dimensions of their work. Teachers are seen not as cultural workers who are busily engaged in reproducing the dominant culture that demonizes and demeans minority cultures, but as "neutral" professionals administering prepackaged programs. Too many statewide testing programs are compatible with this stereotype of teaching and this view of minority students. Macedo (1994) anticipates the kinds of criticisms that often are used to blunt teaching, which tries to overcome such barriers. "A society that remains racist, undemocratic, and discriminatory will not tolerate the transformation of schools and their democratization" (p. 154). We know of no accreditation guidelines that require the kind of crucial reflexivity in the places where teachers work, which view them as sites of contestation and struggle. Such concepts are alien to dominant perspectives in teacher education.

Giroux (1997) has long argued for a different perspective of the role of teacher. First, teachers play a crucial role in perpetuating the social order in the memory, rules, and values that shape their work. Giroux (1997, p. 103) advocates a role of teacher not simply as an intellectual worker who must re-center his/her own authority, which is juxtaposed against that of the state, but as a "transformative intellectual," which means that " [teachers] are also concerned in their teaching with linking empowerment—the ability to think and act critically—to the concept of social transformation."

For a teacher to become the "transformative intellectual" envisioned by Giroux (1980), the teacher must see the curriculum first in nontechnical terms. The view of the curriculum that captures the spirit of becoming a transformative intellectual is that the curriculum represents a social and historical construct, carved out of the experiences of those who wrote it, with the purpose of reproducing a distinctive cultural frame. There is nothing neutral or natural about a curriculum, nor anything remotely similar to standards or other types of benchmarks. In short, there is no science to curriculum development. It is an expression of the political reality available to those engaged in creating it.

The idea that curriculum development is first and foremost a political exercise is an idea foreign to most teacher education programs. "In many respects, teacher education programs have simply not given teachers the conceptual tools they need to view knowledge and problematic, as a historically conditioned, socially constructed phenomenon," says Giroux (1980, p. 155). When prospective teachers are taking their methods courses in "how to teach social studies" or "how to teach math," the instruction consists of technique and appeals to the psychology of learning, that is, to learn how to engage in pedagogical moves that motivate students to acquire the knowledge. There is no effort made to engage prospective teachers in probing hard at the underlying assumptions of knowledge, and almost no penetrating view of classroom discourse as anything but simple technique. Bernstein (1990) has shown how classroom pedagogic practice follows certain rules that relate to social class position of the students. Bernstein divides classroom pedagogic practice into three rules he terms "pedagogic practice as cultural relays" (p. 65). The first rule is *hierarchical*. This rule places the teacher in the role of transmitter and the student in the role of receiver. Acquiring the skills to be a transmitter entails establishing the conditions of order, character, and manner (p. 66). The second set of rules is *sequential*. Everything cannot be taught at once. Some things come first and others later. Sequencing rules imply pacing rules. The third type of rules is called *criterial*. These rules relate to how the learner is to take over and internalize the information and when to apply it. The student has to learn what knowledge is legitimate. Bernstein labels hierarchical rules to the category of regulative rules. The rules of sequencing and pacing are categorized as discursive.

Bernstein then argues that the rules of pacing academic discourse require the cooperation of the home. The home is the second site of knowledge acquisition. Middle-class homes are able to provide such an acquisition site of "pedagogic discipline" (p. 77). Lower-class homes are not as efficient. In schools whose student bodies are comprised of largely lower-class students, the lack of a second site of knowledge acquisition forces the school to "go slower" and emphasize "operations, local skills rather than the exploration of principles and general skills" (p. 77). This serves to weaken the curriculum content. In addition, increasing attention to the academic curriculum de-emphasizes the common language of the lower classes and privileges the language of the social class that controls the school. "In this structure children of the disadvantaged classes are doubly disadvantaged" (p. 78). The teacher education programs that reveal to their students these types of theories are rare in our experience. The proclivity for teacher education students to want the immediate and the most practical and applicable techniques, without any serious study of the underlying assumptions of their future practice, are nearly overwhelming in colleges of education. The so-called hands-on teaching that students want and treasure are not the places where they learn how their pedagogical practices reinforce the socioeconomic status quo. Instead, the failure to learn on the part of lower-class students becomes a story of blaming the laggards with less-than-admirable personal characteristics. Their students' failure to learn is not to be laid at the feet of their teachers or the institutions in which they work, but squarely laid on unmotivated, undisciplined, unappreciative, mentally and culturally inferior students.

A word must also be said about programs that prepare educational leaders. Too often school administrators are trained by giving them the same exposure to technique instead of a thorough grounding in a larger theoretical base, which would open to serious question the notions of organizational efficiency, which are rampant in preparation programs offering courses in budgeting, planning, management, and school law. These programs prepare administrators to become supervisors of teachers, and who remain ignorant of the pedagogic practices that dominate traditional and even alternative schools. The model of schooling which lies behind such courses are those of efficiency rooted in the work of Frederick Taylor and the continuing legacy of scientific management in educational administration (see English, 2000a; Steffy 2000).

The ISLLC standards (Interstate School Leaders Licensure Consortium), sponsored by UCEA (University Council for Educational Administration) beginning in 1985 and supported by foundation funds, had become the guideline for the licensing of school leaders for eight states by 1999. The standards are silent on issues of social justice. They do not take into account how schools work to inhibit their own effectiveness with children of the lowest social classes in the nation. The ISLLC standards emphasize order, control, and technical efficiency. They place school administrators squarely in charge. There is no empowering rationale for communities in any form of social empowerment in the schools licensed by the state.

> The bottom line is that school administrators licensed for practice in the twenty-first century will be the equivalent of secular Jesuits pursuing an ideological agenda that far exceeds the science left behind in the pragmatic pursuit of standards and benchmarks for licensure to practice (English, 2000b, p. 165).

Colleges of education are part of the problem in improving the nation's schools because they are preparing teachers and administrators who are largely ignorant of the roles they play, within institutions that are neither neutral nor sympathetic to ameliorating the social conditions in which the lower class is held in thralldom to the extant socioeconomic order. Although the schools, especially the public schools, have had the challenge to change the status quo, their teachers' and administrators' conceptual and theoretical naivete and lack of alternative grounding in what schools really do to perpetuate the present circumstances mean that they are subject to making the status quo more effective. Not only is the resulting situation tragic, the cost in real dollars and wasted lives is enormous, incalculable, and ultimately unrecoverable.

KEY CONCEPTS OF THIS CHAPTER

Accommodationist approach   The posture towards changing the socioeconomic status quo that rests on the idea of gradualism, a slow process of modification within the existing social arrangements in and out of schools

Alternative assessment   A form of testing that does not involve multiple-choice, paper-and-pencil responses, and which may not be norm-referenced or standardized. Portfolios are often considered a form of alternative assessment.

Bell curve   A frequency distribution of scores on a measuring instrument assumed to be representing a continuous variable (like height and weight). The resultant distribution looks like a bell in which the largest number of responses clusters around the middle. The shape of the distribution is attributed to assumptions of randomness or chance in the population being sampled.

Curricular centered assessment   An approach to assessment that requires a curriculum to be developed first as an anchor to its item content development. As such, the assessment is defined and bordered by the curriculum.

Curricular inclusivity and multiculturalism   A developed curriculum in which the creators understand that using only one curriculum will de-center some alternative cultures. The curriculum is developed and includes these alternative cultures and not in a subordinate way. The viewpoint within the curriculum content is that there are multiple ways of knowing, multiple truths, and multiple notions of what is of value.

De-skilling   First developed by Frederick Taylor in scientific management, the approach consists of taking a complex job and breaking it into simpler components so that a lower level is all that is required to perform the reduced set of tasks.

Educational standards   The establishment of learning or performance statements/expectations that are applied to groups of students clustered in some way, as for example by age level (grade or norm) or by completion of a specific curriculum (Algebra 2).

J curve   A statistical frequency distribution in which the scores are clustered in the top standard deviations of a bell curve; a common distribution for notions of mastery learning in which the largest number of students are very successful in learning a designated curriculum content area.

National curriculum   A curriculum common to all students in the United States, irrespective of state, locality, or demographics. Such a curriculum would be public, open, multicultural, centered on notions of social justice, and move the nation towards eliminating the enormous income gap that is now the norm.

Pedagogic practice   Commonly referred to as the *methods and techniques* used by teachers, but meant in this chapter as including the larger assumptions of professional practice in the context of schooling, which has been prejudiced by race, gender, and social class. An understanding of the linkages between classroom teaching practices and social injustice.

Political context   Refers to the politics of a given context and the distribution of power within that context. The acquisition and allocation of influence within a context is decidedly uneven as it relates to wealth and social class in America.

Reliability   The consistency of measurement over time in regard to a specific testing or assessment instrument

Social justice   Refers to the more equal allocation of wealth and power in the social system, not based on race, gender, sexual preference, or socioeconomic status in the larger society. Dealing with the marginalization of various social groups by the dominant social group and unpacking the agenda of schools to reproduce it in curriculum and pedagogical practice.

Social empowerment approach   A specific attitude towards curriculum construction that is based on the perspective that students and teachers should be empowered within the current system to be active participants in society, as opposed to passive recipients. May involve the learning of the skills of social action and confrontation.

Transformational intellectual   Refers to the role of the classroom teacher, conscious of the power to reinforce the dominant culture, but who challenges that culture to become more inclusive by questioning the sources of domination and refusing to subordinate minority culture and students.

Validity   A multifaceted concept that, when applied to testing, normally refers to whether any test actually measures what it professes to assess. Most often referred to as *face* or *content* validity.

APPLICATIONS

1. Creating a School Profile

Purpose: The purpose of this activity is to create a school profile that is designed to provide staff, students, parents, and the community with information about the school, directly related to its mission.

Often, there is little relationship between public accountability measures regarding school effectiveness and the vision embodied in the school's mission statement. We are assuming here that the school has a mission statement or has adopted the district's mission statement as its own. These mission statements commonly include statements referring to meeting the individual needs of all students, enabling students to think critically, using knowledge to solve complex problems, and providing students with the skills they need to function effectively in a global society. The district's formal assessment system, on the other hand, often assesses basic, low-level skills that require recall of facts, is devoid of challenging problem-solving questions, and requires each student at a designated grade level to take the same assessment.

We are suggesting that teachers and administrators design a school profile that provides information that is directly linked to the mission of the school. For instance, if the students are expected to gain skills to enable them to function effectively in the global society of the future, what information can be collected to document that the necessary skills are being acquired? If the staff believes that the acquisition of a foreign language is a skill that will be required in the future, then the staff should take steps to include foreign language acquisition in the curriculum and assess students' language fluency. Let's assume that all students leaving middle school should be able to converse in Spanish at a level that would enable them to read a newspaper published in Spanish and summarize the article, transcribe a passage from an eighth-grade text, pass a paper-and-pencil test documenting a knowledge base of the Hispanic culture, and be able to hold a conversation in Spanish using vocabulary commonly mastered after completion of Spanish I. Data regarding student achievement for each of these indicators could become part of the information included in a school profile. A pretest for each of these indicators could be prepared and given when students enter middle school. These scores would be recorded. After the post-test was given at the end of eighth grade, it would be possible to show what had been accomplished in terms of student learning over the three-year period.

The same type of procedure could be used to document student growth in the area of technology. The pretest could assess a student's ability to use a word-processing program, such as Word, to be familiar with a presentation program, such as PowerPoint, and to create tables using Excel. By creating pretest assessments to be given by classroom teachers upon entrance to the middle school, teachers, students, and parents would have a clear understanding of what skills students have. These assessments should be given by regularly assigned classroom teachers as part of a planned instructional sequence. In the area of technology, we would expect a wider divergence in students' technology skills.

As you can see, the indicators for determining competence are not hard to identify. By using them as a pretest and post-test for the middle school experience, it is easy to document the substantial learning that has taken place at the middle school. Without this type of documentation, the general public tends to rely on state testing data to judge the quality of the staff, administration, and district.

We advocate the development of a school profile that includes hard data regarding student achievement in all major content areas as it relates to the mission of the school. Multiple measures should be created for each area. These measures should require students to demonstrate the ability to apply, analyze, and evaluate using the knowledge they have learned, acquired at a level clearly understood by teachers, parents and students.

2. Establishing School Benchmarks and Growth Targets

Purpose: To provide schools with concrete targets for improvement that are based on student achievement.

Almost all schools are currently required to develop school-improvement plans. Many times, these plans are consolidated into a district plan and forwarded to the state department for review. In some states, such as Iowa, the state review is part of the database used for continued district accreditation. If the state review shows that the district is not making progress toward specified goals, and the quality of the improvement plans are low, this can trigger a site visit by a state accreditation team. In order to avoid this type of intervention, the school board, in collaboration with the administration, should define what data will be used to specify a baseline, benchmark score for the school. After a benchmark has been established, the board, in collaboration with the district and school administration, should specify the amount of improvement that should occur over time. A school benchmark should include a variety of indicators such as test scores; pretest entry scores compared to post-test exit scores; attendance; and portfolio review. Some of these indicators should be weighted to reflect more importance.

At the present time, few boards have established such a process for defining, tracking, and reporting improvement. Consequently, school improvement plans usually address inputs, such as designing a new program, holding meetings to plan, or documenting information like the number of books in the library. School improvement planning must directly relate to specified student learning and show that the indicators for that learning have improved over time.

With a system like this, the accountability measures for improvement are defined by the local board and are designed by local educators, not the state legislature.

3. Placing District-Written Curriculum and Sample Assessment Measures on the District's Web Site

Purpose: To enable parents and the larger community to have access to information about the board-approved, core curriculum and assessment measures.

The general public, especially parents, is becoming increasingly interested in knowing what students are taught in schools and how achievement is measured. The days when parents were content to trust educators have passed. Presidents, governors, business leaders, and the general public are in favor of more accountability for educators. By placing the district's core curriculum on the its web site, access to this information is available to anyone who wants it. Of course, in order to place the core curriculum on the web, there has to be one. Assuming that there is a core curriculum for all content areas, when it is placed on the web, interested parents can be encouraged to use this information to ensure that students are mastering the indicated skills and knowledge.

When sample test items also appear on the web, parents and students have a better understanding of teacher expectations. For instance, if student achievement in social studies is going to be assessed through a series of short essay responses, students and parents will know that a student will be expected to write in a clear, logical, organized manner. If students being assessed in the area of science are going to be asked to list steps in a process, they will have to be able to think logically and explain clearly. Although both of these types of questions require students to write, they are different writing skills.

The number of homes with one or more computers linked to the Internet is increasing each year. Public libraries and many community service associations make Internet access available to families that cannot afford a computer. Some high schools in the country now require all students to have a portable computer. Arrangements are made for students whose families cannot afford one through scholarships, rentals, or borrowing one from the school. A computer is fast becoming a necessary school supply item.

Access to the district web site will soon be available to every student and parent. Utilizing this availability to disseminate information regarding what students are expected to learn and how they will be assessed is simply good practice. Doing this will eliminate the problem of parents not being informed about expectations, and will enable them to increase their participation as partners with schools.

Once the district's web site includes this information, school web sites can add additional information related to specific classrooms. We know of one district that has mandated that each teacher in the system maintain a web site. Teachers use this web site to post homework assignments, describe units currently being taught, and announce upcoming events.

4. Creating a Study Group to Discuss the Pros and Cons of Establishing a National Curriculum

Purpose: To be proactive with faculty regarding a national curriculum.

Debate over whether to establish a national curriculum is a hot topic among politicians across the country. Practicing educators at the local level need to engage in the debate and help inform the politicians about the issues involved and the impact of having or not having a national curriculum.

In order to create an informed local constituency within the district, we recommend that study groups exploring this topic be formed. The study group should operate with a charge from the administration to study the topic, identify the strengths and weaknesses of such a move, and prepare a position paper to be used for system-wide discussion and debate.

By debating the issue and taking a position, local educators must come to grips with how curriculum and accountability will be addressed within the district in the future. If there is no national curriculum, then does the group take the position that there should be a state curriculum and accountability mechanism, or do local educators believe there should be a local curriculum and accountability mechanism? It is no longer acceptable that there is no formal curriculum or accountability mechanism at any level. In reality, there is probably responsibility for curriculum and assessment at all levels. Understanding the implications and strengths and weaknesses of varying positions can result in a better delineation of responsibilities for the creation of curriculum and the assessment mechanism needed to assess it.

5. Drafting Legislation to Improve Education

Purpose: To enable local educators to understand how to improve public education through the legislative process.

Many state legislatures are considering statutes regarding social promotion, class size, pay for performance, vouchers, charter schools, and sanctions and rewards. Each of these bills could have a dramatic impact on the lives of teachers, administrators, and children. Rather than waiting until the legislation has passed to deal with the implications, we suggest a proactive approach. Establish focus groups in the system to study each of these topics and draft proposed legislation to deal with the issues involved.

Each focus group should begin by becoming informed about the status of legislation across the country on this issue. Legislation in one state is often enacted, with only minor changes, in another state. The Education Commission of the States is the organization that tracks legislation nationally. Contact with this organization should enable the focus group to gather a multitude of information on the topic, including what states have enacted statutes, what studies have been done, and what the impact of the legislation has been. Armed with this information, the focus group should next find out the status of proposed legislation in their state. This could be done through contact with the staff supporting the legislators, the legislative representatives from the major educational organizations, or discussion with legislators serving on the Education Committee. Discussions with local legislators can also be helpful in determining the extent of support for legislation in a given area. It may be possible to get copies of previous proposed legislation. Reviewing these proposed statutes and reading the minutes of meetings where they were discussed can also be helpful.

Armed with the national and state perspectives, the focus group participants may want to begin to draft proposed legislation. The group may decide it wants to solicit input from more stakeholders on the topic. This could lead to surveys of parents, faculty, or a broader community. After the legislation is drafted, the focus group will want to meet the administration and the board to discuss it. The board and administration may decide that they want to sponsor a legislative breakfast and present the proposed legislation at that meeting. At the very least, this effort will inform educators in the system about the topic, show legislators that educators are well informed on the topic, and heighten the awareness of the local legislators regarding how local educators feel about the topic. It is a win–win situation all the way around.

6. Developing a Social Justice Curriculum

Purpose: To accept the responsibility for teaching students how to promote social justice.

By consciously preparing a written curriculum dealing with social justice, educators are making a statement about the role of the school in promoting a better society. Although social justice issues have traditionally been studied in schools, we envision this document becoming one that would bring the topic front and center. We envision this curriculum as being interdisciplinary, although much of the content might typically fall into the area of social studies.

The process could begin by taking current curriculum guides and identifying where social justice issues are currently being addressed. By identifying the themes and patterns already in the curriculum, it may be possible to simply develop strands to be covered, and add student outcomes where necessary.

Because this is a sensitive area, educators would want to be sure that present board policy and the district's mission and goal statements incorporate teaching these skills. If they do not, further discussion with the board may be needed. We realize that all school districts may not presently be interested in this idea. However, if our society is to move toward a more socially just one, we believe there is a role for the school in achieving this.

7. Working with Local Colleges and Universities to Infuse Social Empowerment into Teacher and Administrator Training Programs

Purpose: To provide teachers and administrators with the skills they will need to effectively advocate and teach concepts related to social justice.

Most teacher and administrator training programs do not address social empowerment skills, even though the Interstate School Leaders Licensure Consortium (ISLLC) has identified this area as one of its six standards for initial and continued licensure of administrators. K–12 faculty and administrators should be working closely with higher education faculty to establish a collaborative committee to discuss how colleges of education can change to support social empowerment of teachers and administrators, and provide them with the skills necessary to act as transformative intellectuals.

REFERENCES

Adams, J., Jr., and Kirst, M. (1999). New demands and concepts for educational accountability: Striving for results in an era of excellence. In J. Murphy and K. Louis (eds.) *Handbook of research on educational administration*, 463–490, San Francisco, CA: Jossey-Bass.

Alinsky, S. (1969). *Reveille for radicals*. New York: Vintage.

Alinsky, S. (1972). *Rules for radicals: A pragmatic primer for realistic radicals*. New York: Vintage.

Baringer, P. (2000, August 15). Fundamental disagreement. Letter to the Editor. *The Wall Street Journal*, A27.

Bates, S. (1993). *Battleground: One mother's crusade, the religious right, and the struggle for control of our classrooms.* New York: Poseidon.

Bernstein, B. (1990). *The structuring of pedagogic discourse: Vol. 4, class, codes and control.* London: Routledge & Kegan Paul.

Brooks, G., and Horwitz, T. (2000, August 21). As Olympics loom, Australians agonize over Aborigine issues. *The Wall Street Journal,* 236 (35), A1–8.

Bosworth, A. (1967). *America's concentration camps.* New York: Norton.

Callahan, R. (1962). *The cult of efficiency.* Chicago: University of Chicago Press.

Carlson, D. (1993). Literacy and urban school reform. In C. Lankshear and P. McLaren (eds.) *Critical literacy: politics, praxis, and the postmodern,* 217–246. Albany: SUNY Press.

Carnoy, M. (1999). Globalization and educational reform: What planners need to know. Paris, France: UNESCO, International Institute for Educational Planning.

Carter, T. (1970). *Mexican Americans in school: a history of educational neglect.* Princeton, NJ: Educational Testing Service.

Chen, J. (1980). *The Chinese of America.* San Francisco, CA: Harper and Row.

Cheney, L. (1994, October 20). The end of history. *The Wall Street Journal,* A26 (W), A22 (E).

Claycomb, C., and Kysilko, D. (2000, Spring). The purposes and elements of effective assessment systems. *The State Education Standard* 1 (2), 7–11.

Cole, M. (1977). Culture, cognition, and IQ testing. In P. Houts (ed.) *The myth of measurability.* New York: Hart, 116–123.

Daniels, R. (1974). *The politics of prejudice: The anti-Japanese movement in California and the struggle for Japanese exclusion.* New York: Atheneum.

Darder, A. (1991). *Culture and power in the classroom.* New York: Bergin and Garvey.

Davis, D. (1975). *The problem of slavery in the age of revolution 1770–1823.* Ithaca, NY: Cornell University Press.

Delgado-Gaitan, C., and Trueba, H. (1991). *Crossing cultural borders: Education for immigrant families in America.* London: Falmer.

Donaldson, K., and Seepe, S. (1999, October). Antiracist education and curriculum transformation for equity and justice in the new millennium: United States and South African challenges. *International Journal of Educational Reform* 8 (4), 326–341.

Douglas, W. (1966). *The Bible and the schools.* Boston, MA: Little, Brown.

DuBois, P., Eaton, M., Garet, M., and Miller, M. (2000, April). Study design and initial findings for a national evaluation of projects funded by the magnet schools assistance program. Unpublished paper, American Education Research Association, New Orleans, LA.

Eaton, W. (1990). The vulnerability of school superintendents: The thesis reconsidered. In W. Eaton (ed.) *Shaping the superintendency: A reexamination of Callahan and the cult of efficiency,* 11–35. New York: Teachers College Press,

English, F. (2000a, April). Does the ghost of Frederick Taylor haunt the ISLLC-standards? Unpublished paper, American Education Research Association, New Orleans, LA.

English, F. (2000b). Psst! What does one call a set of non-empirical beliefs required to be accepted on faith and enforced by authority? [Answer: a religion, aka the ISLLC standards]. *International Journal of Leadership in Education* 3 (2), 159–167.

Fine, B. (1975). *The stranglehold of the I.Q.* Garden City, NY: Doubleday.

Firestone, W., Fitz, J., and Broadfoot, P. (1999, Winter). Power, learning, and legitimation: Assessment implementation across levels in the United States and the United Kingdom. *American Educational Research Journal* 36 (4), 759–793.

Fiske, E., and Ladd, H. (2000, May 17). A distant laboratory: Learning cautionary lessons from New Zealand's schools. *Education Week* 29 (36), 38, 56.

Forney, M. (2000, August 24). Chinese suing Japanese firms hope to find justice in the U.S. *The Wall Street Journal*, A19.

Gandhi, M. (1948). *Gandhi's autobiography: The story of my experiments with truth.* M. Desai (trans.). Washington, DC: Public Affairs Press.

Giroux, H. (1997). *Border crossings: Cultural workers and the politics of education.* New York: Routledge & Kegan Paul.

Giroux, H. (1980). *Ideology, culture, and the process of schooling.* Philadelphia, PA: Temple University Press.

Glasser, I. (2000, July 31). *Newsletter*, ACLU Guardians of Liberty. New York: ACLU.

Gramsci, A. (1971). *Selections from a prison notebook.* In Q. Hoare and G. Smith (eds. and trans.) New York: International.

Gutierrez, K., and Larson, J. (1994, January). Language borders: Recitation as hegemonic discourse. *International Journal of Educational Reform* 3 (1), 22–36.

Haertel, E. (1994). Theoretical and practical implications. In T. Guskey (ed.) *High-stakes performance assessment*, 65–76. Thousand Oaks, CA: Corwin Press.

Horwitt, S. (1989). *Let them call me rebel.* New York: Knopf.

Jensen, A. (1980). *Bias in mental testing.* New York: Free Press.

Jordan, W. (1968). *White over black: American attitudes toward the negro, 1550–1812.* Chapel Hill: University of North Carolina Press.

Kahne, J., and Bailey, K. (1999, Fall). The role of social capital in youth development: The case of 'I have a dream' programs. *Educational Evaluation and Policy Analysis* 21 (3), 321–343.

Kanigel, R. (1997). *The one best way: Frederick Winslow Taylor and the enigma of efficiency.* New York: Viking.

Kluger, R. (1975). *Simple justice: The history of Brown v. board of education and black America's struggle for equality.* New York: Vintage.

Kohn, A. (2000). *The case against standardized testing: Raising the scores, ruining the schools.* Westport, CT: Heinemann.

Kronholz, J. (2000, September 13). Statewide high school graduation tests favored by most parents, poll indicates. *The Wall Street Journal*, A2.

LaBelle, T. and Ward, C. (1994). *Multiculturalism and education: Diversity and its impact on schools and society.* Albany: SUNY Press.

Levy, J. (1975). *Cesar Chavez: Autobiography of la causa.* New York: Norton.

Lisovskaya, E. (1999, July). International influences on private education in Russia: the case of St. Petersburg, 1991–1998. *International Journal of Educational Reform* 8 (3), 206–218.

Lynch, P. (1999, August 6). NCPEA's history and role in preparing administrators of schools for Mexican American people. Unpublished paper.

Macedo, D. (1994). *Literacies of power: What Americans are not allowed to know.* Boulder, CO: Westview.

Manatt, R. (1995). *When right is wrong: Fundamentalists and the public schools.* Lancaster, PA: Technomic.

Matthiessen, P. (1969). *Sal si puedes: Cesar Chavez and the new American revolution.* New York: Random House.

McLaren, P. (1997). Fashioning *los olvidados* in the age of cynical reason. In P. McLaren (ed.) *Revolutionary multiculturalism: Pedagogies of dissent for the new millennium.* Boulder, CO: Westview.

Mirande, A., and Enriquez, E. (1979). *La Chicana: the Mexican-American woman.* Chicago: University of Chicago Press.

Montejano, D. (1987). *Anglos and Mexicans in the making of Texas, 1836–1986.* Austin: University of Texas Press.

Musick, M. (2000, September 6). Show us the test. *Education Week* 20 (1), 63, 84.

Nash, G., Crabtree, C., and Dunn, R. (1997). *History on trial.* New York: Knopf.

Neill, M. (2000, Spring). State exams flunk test of quality. *The State Education Standard* 1 (2), 31–35.

Numbers, R. (1992). *The creationists: The evolution of scientific creationism.* Berkeley: University of California Press.

Osofsky, G. (1967). *The burden of race.* New York: HarperCollins.

Owen, D. (1985). *None of the above: Behind the myth of scholastic aptitude.* Boston: Houghton Mifflin.

Penniman, B. (2000, Spring). After great expectations, hard times: Why assessment in Massachusetts undermines the early promise of education reform. *The State Education Standard* 1 (2), 23–26.

Phillips, M. (2000, September 13). World bank rethinks strategy for poor. *The Wall Street Journal*, A2.

Popkewitz, T. (2000, January–February). The denial of change in educational change: Systems of ideas in the construction of national policy and evaluation. *Educational Researcher* 29 (1), 17–29.

Popper, K. (1968). *The logic of scientific discovery.* New York: Harper and Row.

Pruyn, M. (1994, January). Becoming subjects through critical practice: How students in one elementary classroom critically read and wrote their world. *International Journal of Educational Reform* 3 (1), 37–50.

Purvin, G. (1977). The hidden agendas of IQ. In P. Houts (ed.) *The myth of measurability.* New York: Hart, 106–115.

Reich, R. (2000, September 6). The case for 'progressive' vouchers. *The Wall Street Journal,* A26.

Reinhart, B. (1999). *In the middle of a muddle: How not to reinvent government.* Vienna, VA: Manta Press.

Sacks, P. (1999). *Standardized minds: The high price of America's testing culture and what we can do to change it.* Cambridge, MA: Perseus Books.

Sapon-Shevin, M. (1994). *Playing favorites: Gifted education and the disruption of community.* Albany: SUNY Press.

Servin, M. (1974). *An awakened minority: The Mexican-Americans.* Beverly Hills, CA: Glencoe Press.

Sleeter, C., and Grant, C. (1988). *Making choices for multicultural education: Five approaches to race, class and gender.* Columbus, OH: Merrill

Schmidt, W., McKnight, C., and Raizen, S. (1996). *A splintered vision: An investigation of U.S. science and mathematics education.* East Lansing, MI: U.S. National Research Center.

Steffy, B. (2000, April). The ISLLC standards as the rational-technical apparatus of-state/university/professional control of educational leadership. Unpublished paper, American Education Research Association, New Orleans, LA.

Steffy, B. (1993). *The Kentucky education reform. Lessons for America.* Lancaster, PA: Technomic.

Steinberg, J. (2000, September 3). Nation's schools struggling to find enough principals. *New York Times,* 1, 16.

The Economist. (1998, June 20). The Tijuana triangle. 13–14.

Tucker, M., and Codding, J. (1998). *Standards for our schools.* San Francisco, CA: Jossey-Bass.

Tyack, D. (1974). *The one best system: A history of American urban education.* Cambridge, MA: Harvard University Press.

Wilkins, J. (2000, April). Characteristics of demographic opportunity structures and their relationship to school-level achievement: the case of Virginia's standards of learning. Unpublished paper, American Education Research Association, New Orleans, LA.

Author Index

Subject Index

About the Authors

$\mathcal{F}$enwick W. English is a professor of education in the Department of Educational Leadership and Policy Studies in the College of Education at Iowa State University, Ames, Iowa. He has been a professor at Lehigh University, the University of Cincinnati, and the University of Kentucky. He has served as a major platform speaker for many national education associations, and has presented symposium papers at the University Council for Educational Administration (UCEA) and Division A of the American Education Research Association (AERA). His practitioner experience includes a middle school principalship; assistant superintendent in Sarasota, Florida; and a superintendency in New York. He is the author/coauthor of twenty books. He earned his B.S. and M.S. from the University of Southern California and his Ph.D. from Arizona State University.

Betty E. Steffy is a professor of education in the Department of Educational Leadership and Policy Studies in the College of Education at Iowa State University, Ames, Iowa. She was a dean of a School of Education at a regional campus of Purdue University, Indiana, and served as Deputy Superintendent of Instruction in the Kentucky Department of Education during the early years of the implementation of the Kentucky Education Reform Act (KERA). Her practitioner experience includes a team leader at an elementary school; Director of Curriculum for an intermediate educational agency in the Pittsburgh, Pennsylvania region; an assistant superintendent of schools of Lynbrook, New York; and a superintendent of schools in Moorestown, New Jersey. She is the author/coauthor of ten prior books in education and symposium papers at UCEA and AERA. She earned her B.A., M.A.T., and Ed.D. from the University of Pittsburgh.